Warrior • 38

Fallschirmjäger

German Paratrooper 1935–45

Bruce Quarrie • Illustrated by Velimir Vuksic

First published in Great Britain in 2001 by Osprey Publishing,
Midland House, West Way, Botley, Oxford OX2 0PH, UK
44-02 23rd St, Suite 219, Long Island City, NY 11101, USA
E-mail: info@ospreypublishing.com

Transferred to digital print on demand 2010

First published 2001
7th impression 2008

Printed and bound by PrintOnDemand-Worldwide.com, Peterborough, UK

A CIP catalogue record for this book is available from the British Library

ISBN: 978 1 84176 326 2

Editor: Nikolai Bogdanovic
Design: Ken Vail Graphic Design, Cambridge, UK
Index by Alison Worthington
Originated by Magnet Harlequin, Uxbridge, UK

Artist's Note

Readers may care to note that the original paintings from which the colour plates in this book were prepared are available for private
sale. All reproduction copyright whatsoever is retained by the Publishers. All enquiries should be addressed to:

Velimir Vuksic, Ilica 54, 10000 Zagreb, Croatia

The Publishers regret that they can enter into no correspondence upon this matter.

Editor's Note

The notes referred to in the text can be found on page 55.

Photo Credits

Author's collection: pp.10, 28 top, 43, 44, 45 top, 46, 47 bottom, 50. *Der Adler* (Luftwaffe wartime magazine): pp.20 top left, 21, 23
bottom, 24, 26, 48. Gavin Cadden: p.16. *Signaal* (Wehrmacht wartime magazine): p.62. All other photos are courtesy of Christopher
Ailsby Historical Archives.

FOR A CATALOGUE OF ALL BOOKS PUBLISHED BY OSPREY
MILITARY AND AVIATION PLEASE CONTACT:

Osprey Direct, c/o Random House Distribution Center,
400 Hahn Road, Westminster, MD 21157
Email: uscustomerservice@ospreypublishing.com

Osprey Direct, The Book Service Ltd, Distribution Centre,
Colchester Road, Frating Green, Colchester, Essex, CO7 7DW
E-mail: customerservice@ospreypublishing.com

www.ospreypublishing.com

CONTENTS

FALLSCHIRMJÄGER GERMAN PARATROOPER 1935–45

INTRODUCTION

'You are the chosen fighting men of the Wehrmacht. You will seek combat and train yourselves to endure all hardships. Battle shall be your fulfilment.'

From Adolf Hitler's
'Ten Commandments' to the Fallschirmtruppen.

The idea of airborne troops is far from new and dates back at least to the ancient Greek legend of the warrior Bellerophon riding into battle on the winged horse Pegasus. Even parachutes, as toys modelled on parasols, have existed for centuries, but it was not until the late 19th century that the idea of a 'chute without a rigid framework evolved. The First World War brought the concept to maturity as a life-saving device, first for observation balloon crews and then for those of heavier-than-air machines. Early types were of the static line variety, in which a rope attached to the aircraft pulls the parachute out of its container. The ripcord, which proved a major benefit for pilots and other aircrew, was not invented until 1919. However, the static line variety came back into its own when the concept of parachute troopers began to mature.

The first serious parachute experiments were conducted by the Russians and Italians. Many German observers were interested, even excited, but, bound by the terms of the Treaty of Versailles, which forbade reconstruction of an air force, they were forced to dream. However, when Adolf Hitler was confirmed as Chancellor, the dreamers and schemers began to work more openly towards their goals. Once he repudiated the hated Versailles Treaty and re-introduced conscription, all restrictions on their ambitions were removed, and few men were more ambitious than the former First World War 'Richthofen' Staffel fighter pilot ace Hermann Göring, who quickly rose to command the reconstituted *Luftwaffe* (Air Force).

Göring had been amongst those who watched Russian paratroop demonstration exercises in 1931 and 1935, and he had been so impressed that he now decided to begin construction of a German parachute corps. He already had a tiny nucleus of paratroops in the former Prussian police Regiment 'General Göring', and in October 1936 he arranged a demonstration jump to encourage volunteers to form a parachute rifle battalion within this regiment. Although the demonstration was inauspicious, since one of the 36 jumpers injured himself on landing and had to be carried off on a stretcher, Göring soon had the necessary 600 recruits for his battalion. In 1938 the battalion was transferred to the embryo 7 *Flieger* (Airborne) Division[1]. Further expansion was steady and, by the time general mobilisation for war was ordered in August 1939, the Luftwaffe had two full parachute rifle battalions with support troops as the nucleus of this first German airborne division. The army (*Heer*), meanwhile, had a full infantry division specially trained in air-landing techniques.

The difference between paratroops (*Fallschirmtruppen*) and air-landing troops (*Luftlandetruppen*) is simple. The former are trained to jump by parachute or land by glider to seize important tactical objectives such as airfields or bridges ahead of advancing ground forces, holding them until relieved. Paratroops are classed as light infantry (*Jäger*) and do not have much in the way of heavy weapons nor an inexhaustible supply of ammunition, so relief must be swift. Enter the air-landing soldier, flown with heavier equipment in transport aircraft such as the Junkers Ju 52, to land on ground already seized by the paratroops and deploy rapidly in their support.

But, if paratroops are so vulnerable to counter-attack by conventional forces, with artillery and tanks, why bother with them at all? The kernel of the answer lies in the fact that most decisive battles are won through a combination of speed, surprise and shock and not necessarily through superior numbers in men or *matériel*. Outflanking or, even better, getting behind the enemy's lines and attacking him from the rear, have always been the best, quickest and least costly means of winning.

Under normal circumstances, soldiers regard what lies in front of them as the enemy and what lies behind as friendly. Paratroops change that through what has been aptly called 'vertical envelopment'. Even a relatively small force of men landed behind the lines causes everyone to look over their shoulders rather than concentrating on their front. The knowledge that a foe lies behind you causes disproportionate apprehension, saps morale and draws off reserves which could otherwise be deployed elsewhere more effectively[2]. Moreover, there are never sufficient reserves to guard every possible objective against airborne assault, so paratroops can normally expect to gain at least a temporary numerical advantage. In the first couple of years of the Second World War, it was this knowledge that the Germans exploited so successfully with the *Blitzkrieg* (Lightning War) concept, to which the Fallschirmtruppen were an inspired adjunct. So inspired, in fact, that both America and Britain, which had been woefully slow in appreciating the value of airborne forces, went into top gear to create their own after the 1940 campaigns.

Prior to the almost total success of paratroop and air-landing operations in April and May 1940, however, there were doubters even in Germany, and there was considerable disagreement between the Luftwaffe and the Heer as to how the new airborne forces should best be deployed. Generally speaking, the air force pundits thought they should merely be used in relatively small numbers as saboteurs to disrupt enemy lines of communication, spread panic and delay the arrival of reserves at the front. Many army officers, on the other hand, believed in their employment *en masse* to create an instant bridgehead in a location the enemy would not be expecting. In the end, of course, both tactics would be employed during the war, proving only that each side was equally right.

CHRONOLOGY

1933
January — Adolf Hitler sworn in as German Chancellor.
February — Hermann Göring, as head of the Prussian police force, forms the Berlin-based *Polizeiabteilung* (Police Detachment) 'Wecke', which includes a small parachute-trained air section (*Luftaufsicht*) for special operations.

1934
July — Polizeiabteilung 'Wecke' renamed *Landespolizeigruppe* (Provincial Police Group) 'Wecke'.

1935
February — Accompanying renunciation of the Treaty of Versailles, the Luftwaffe is brought into existence headed by Reichsmarschall Göring.
March — Hitler re-introduces general conscription. Landespolizeigruppe 'Wecke' renamed LPG 'General Göring'.
October — LPG 'General Göring' transferred from police to Luftwaffe control. Its CO is now Oberstleutnant Friedrich Jakoby.

1936
January — LPG 'General Göring' renamed Regiment 'General Göring'. An Order of the Day from General der Luftwaffe Erhard Milch officially inaugurates a German parachute corps and volunteers are called for to establish a *Fallschirmschützen Bataillon* (Parachute Rifle Battalion). Training begins at Döberitz and Altengrabow.
Summer — OKH (*Oberkommando des Heeres*, or Army High Command) also calls for volunteers for a new *Schwere-Fallschirm-Infanterie Kompanie* (Heavy Parachute Infantry Company) to be formed at Stendal.

1937
Central Parachute School (*Fallschirmschule*) created at Stendal under Major Gerhard Bassenge. DFS 230 glider enters production.

1938
April — Fallschirmschützen Bataillon detached from Regiment 'General Göring' to become I Bataillon, 1 Fallschirmjäger Regiment (I/FJR 1), at Stendal (Major Bruno Bräuer). At the same time the Schwere-Fallschirm-Infanterie Kompanie is expanded to a battalion (Major Richard Heidrich) based in Braunschweig.
July — Generalmajor Kurt Student given responsibility for forming 7 Flieger Division based at Stendal with headquarters at Tempelhof.

1939
January — Student appointed *Inspekteur der Fallschirm-und-Luftlandetruppen* (Inspector of Parachute and Air-Landing Troops). Heidrich's Army parachute battalion absorbed by the Luftwaffe as II Bataillon, 1 Fallschirmjäger Regiment (II/FJR 1). Army pride salvaged by retention of Generalleutnant Graf Hans von Sponeck's 22 Luftlande Division. Elements of this unit fought in Belgium and Holland in 1940, and the division as a whole saw action in Russia in 1941–42 before it was assigned to occupation duty on Crete until late 1944. At the end of the war it fought and surrendered in Yugoslavia.
August — Approval given to begin raising a third battalion for 1 Fallschirmjäger Regiment (III/FJR 1) and a second regiment (FJR 2), all as part of 7 Flieger Division.
September — Elements of II/ and III/FJR 1 fight in a ground role during the invasion of Poland.
November — Student begins forming *Sturmabteilung* (Assault Detachment) 'Koch' from elements of I/ and II/FJR 1 (Hauptmann Walter Koch) in great secrecy at Hildesheim for the assault on the Belgian fortress of Eben Emael and bridges over the Albert Canal.

1940
April — **Denmark**: Nr. 4 Kompanie of I/FJR 1 captures the two Aalborg airfields and Vordingborg bridge in Copenhagen. **Norway**: Nr. 2 Kompanie seizes Fornebu airfield outside Oslo, while Nr. 3 Kompanie helps capture Sola airfield at Stavanger. Nr. 1 Kompanie, dropped further north in the

Gudbrandsalen valley, is forced to surrender by British troops after running out of ammunition.

May **Norway**: I/FJR 1 drops at Narvik too late to prevent the British evacuation. **Holland**: The balance of FJR 1, excluding Sturmabteilung 'Koch', and FJR 2, capture the Dordrecht and Moerdijk bridges on the approaches to Rotterdam and the airfields at Ockenburg, Valkenburg, Waalhaven and Ypenburg. **Belgium**: The fortress of Eben Emael and the bridges at Kanne, Veldwezelt and Vroenhoven are successfully assaulted by the four sections of Sturmabteilung 'Koch' and held until the Fallschirmtruppen are relieved.

1941

April **Greece**: FJR 2 (Oberst Albert Sturm) successfully cuts off British Empire troops retreating into the Peloponnese across the Corinth Canal.

May **Crete**: Kurt Student, who had been promoted to General der Luftwaffe, now commands XI *Fliegerkorps* (Airborne Corps). Command of 7 Flieger Division passes to Generalleutnant Wilhelm Süßmann. FJR 1 (Bräuer), FJR 2 (Sturm) and FJR 3 (Heidrich) are complemented by the descendant of Hauptmann (now Major) Koch's 1940 Sturmabteilung, expanded into the *Luftlande-Sturm* (Air-landing Assault) Regiment under Generalmajor Eugen Meindl; Koch commands its I Bataillon. Glider-borne and parachute assaults are launched in two waves against the three airfields of Máleme, Retimo and Heraklion. They are closely followed by air- and sea-landed troops of Generalmajor Julius Ringel's 5 *Gebirgs* (Mountain) Division. The invasion succeeds only at very heavy cost to the Fallschirmtruppen, including the death of General Süßmann, effectively nipping in the bud any future major airborne operations. Henceforth, for the most part, the paratroops fight as elite infantry.

September **Russia**: 2nd Battalion of Meindl's Sturmregiment precedes the bulk of 7 Flieger Division (now commanded by Generalleutnant Petersen) to the Leningrad front.

December Oberst Alfred Sturm's reinforced FJR 2 (*Kampfgruppe* [Battlegroup] 'Sturm') is sent to the Ukraine, while the remainder of 7 Flieger Division is pulled back to Stendal for a rest after sustaining heavy losses.

1942

March Göring orders Regiment 'General Göring' be expanded into Fallschirm Brigade 'Hermann Göring' (Oberst Paul Conrath).

August **Africa**: After Student's plan for an airborne invasion of Malta is abandoned in July, the new, specially formed, Fallschirm Brigade 'Ramcke', commanded by Generalmajor Bernhard Ramcke, is flown to Tobruk to bolster the Afrika Korps' drive on the Suez Canal and Cairo.

October **Russia**: After recuperating in France, 7 Flieger Division is posted to the Smolensk front and renamed 1 Fallschirm Division; command passes to Richard Heidrich, now Generalmajor.

November **Egypt/Libya**: 'Ramcke' Brigade renamed 2 Fallschirm Brigade. After being cut off during the retreat from El Alamein, and lacking transport, 600 survivors march cross-country to rejoin Rommel's forces. **Tunisia**: Following Allied landings in French North-West Africa, further Fallschirmtruppen airlifted into Tunisia to reinforce *Armeegruppe* (Army Group) 'Afrika'. They include Major Walter Koch's FJR 5.

1943

January Fallschirm Brigade 'Hermann Göring' begins expansion to become Fallschirm Division 'HG' with Paul Conrath promoted to Generalmajor, and two battalions precede the remainder to Tunisia.

March–April After heavy fighting, especially at Medjez-el-Bab and Tebourba, the Fallschirmtruppen, including the remnants of Ramcke's Brigade but excluding most of the men of the fledgling 'HG' Division, are amongst those evacuated before the final collapse in Tunisia. At the same time, 1 Fallschirm Division and Kampfgruppe 'Sturm' are brought back from Russia. Ramcke's and Sturm's brigades form the nucleus of a new 2 Fallschirm Division commanded by Ramcke. Göring also begins an immediate reconstruction of 1 Fallschirm and the 'HG' Divisions; the latter is sent to Sicily to help repel the expected invasion. Similarly, a new 5 Fallschirm Division begins forming in France around a cadre of XI

	Fliegerkorps' *Lehr* (Demonstration) Bataillon; it is commanded by Generalmajor Gustav Wilke.
July	**Sicily**: Immediately after the Allied invasion of Sicily, FJR 3 and 4 are airlifted in to reinforce the 'HG' Division. Main fighting around Catania airfield and Primasole Bridge, with 'HG' in the Gela sector. Ramcke's 2 Fallschirm Division moves from France to the outskirts of Rome. Mussolini overthrown and put under house arrest. Marshal Pietro Badoglio takes over the government.
August	Sicily evacuated.
September	**Italy**: Allied forces invade and Badoglio signs the armistice. 1 Fallschirm Division opposes British Eighth Army landings at Foggia; 2 Fallschirm Division occupies Rome and disarms its garrison. 'HG' Division spearheads counter-attack against US Fifth Army beachhead at Salerno before falling back slowly through Sorrento and Naples. In an unprecedented operation, Hitler commissions SS-*Hauptsturmführer* (Captain) Otto Skorzeny to rescue Mussolini from imprisonment in a hotel on the Gran Sasso plateau in the Apennine Mountains. Men of FJR 7 land in DFS 230 gliders, free him, and he is flown to safety.
October	3 Fallschirm Division (Generalmajor Richard Schimpf) begins forming in France around a cadre from FJR 1. 'HG' Division taken out of the line to rest at Cassino. During this period Oberstleutnant Julius Schlegel is responsible for removing the Monte Cassino monastery treasures to safety in Rome.
November	4 Fallschirm Division (Generalmajor Heinrich Trettner) begins forming in Italy around a nucleus from 2 Fallschirm Division. It includes pro-fascist Italian paratroops. **Russia**: 2 Fallschirm Division, temporarily commanded by Gustav Wilke, posted to the Zhitomir front.
December	2 Fallschirm Division airlifted to Kirovgrad and takes heavy casualties during the subsequent fighting retreat to west of the River Dniestr.
1944	
January	**Italy**: 1 and 4 Fallschirm Divisions fall under the aegis of the new I Fallschirmkorps commanded by General der Luftwaffe Alfred Schlemm. 'HG' and 4 Fallschirm Divisions now spearhead the counter-attack against the new Allied beachhead at Anzio which threatens to outflank the Gustav Line.
February	1 Fallschirm Division takes up the defence of Cassino and Monte Cassino.
March–April	Heidrich's men repulse all Allied attempts to take the Cassino positions. 'HG' Division taken out of the line to rest again and renamed 1 Fallschirm-Panzer Division 'HG', now commanded by Generalmajor Wilhelm Schmalz.
May	'HG' Division rushed into another counter-attack when the Allies break out of the Anzio beachhead, but is forced to fall back through Rome. The commander of German forces in Italy, Feldmarschall Albert Kesselring, finally orders the Cassino position evacuated. **France**: Survivors of 2 Fallschirm Division are repatriated to Germany, where Ramcke resumes command and Wilke returns to 5 Fallschirm Division, which is now in Brittany alongside 3 Fallschirm Division as part of General Eugen Meindl's II Fallschirmkorps. **Yugoslavia**: In an abortive attempt to kill or capture the partisan leader Tito, 500 SS-Fallschirmjäger Bataillon lands by parachute and glider near his headquarters outside Drvar. However, Tito is not even there and more numerous partisan forces soon drive off the invaders.
June	**Italy**: Rome falls. 1 Fallschirm Division transferred to the Adriatic sector, now commanded by Generalmajor Karl-Lothar Schulz because Heidrich takes over I Fallschirmkorps. The division retreats slowly to the Gothic Line. **France**: Allied forces land in Normandy. The only Fallschirmjäger unit immediately facing them is Major Friedrich Freiherr von der Heydte's FJR 6; the remainder of 2 Fallschirm Division is still refitting at Köln-Wahn but is rushed to join II Fallschirmkorps in Brittany. Ramcke is given command of the defence of Brest and Oberst Hans Kroh takes over the division. Von der Heydte's men give the US 101st Airborne a hard time around Carentan for four days before falling back. Meanwhile,

	II Fallschirmkorps moves to Normandy with 3 Fallschirm Division in the St Lô sector and 5 Fallschirm Division outside Caen. An embryo 6 Fallschirm Division (Generalleutnant Rüdiger von Heyking) begins forming in northern France.
July	3 Fallschirm Division takes and inflicts heavy casualties during the battle for St Lô and Schimpf is wounded. 5 Fallschirm Division also heavily engaged. 'HG' Division is pulled out of Italy, and after a brief refit is posted to the Warsaw front.
August	Bulk of 3 and 5 Fallschirm Divisions trapped and decimated in the Falaise Pocket while 6 Fallschirm Division battles in front of Paris. Allies lay siege to Brest, defended principally by 2 Fallschirm Division. **Poland**: 'HG' Division falls back behind River Vistula.
September	Ramcke finally surrenders Brest and enters American captivity. 6 Fallschirm Division trapped in the Mons Pocket and reduced to two battalions. Nevertheless, they take part in the counter-attacks in Holland as part of Student's new First Fallschirm Armee alongside the newly created 7 Fallschirm Division (Generalleutnant Wolfgang Erdmann). The latter formation significantly delays British XXX Corps in its drive to relieve the paratroops in Arnhem.
October	**Eastern Front**: Göring orders expansion of the 'HG' Division into a Korps consisting of 1 and 2 Fallschirm-Panzer Divisions under Oberst Hans Horst von Necker and Oberst Erich Walter respectively. Both divisions are weaker than the parent formation and are forced to fall back into East Prussia. **Western Front**: 3 and 5 Fallschirm Divisions, while being rehabilitated in Germany principally to take part in Hitler's grandiose Ardennes offensive, are meanwhile committed to action against Allied forces in Holland and Alsace respectively. A new 2 Fallschirm Division (Generalleutnant Walther Lackner) is constructed and later fights in Holland, the Reichswald and during the battle for the Rhein crossings.
December	3 and 5 Fallschirm Divisions are rebuilt again and form part of Sixth Panzer and Seventh Armees for the Ardennes' offensive. The latter division, now commanded by Generalmajor Ludwig Heilmann, achieves initial objectives and plays a significant role in delaying Patton's Third Army as it struggles to relieve Bastogne. 3 Fallschirm Division (now Generalleutnant Karl Wadehn), accompanying SS-Kampfgruppe 'Peiper', fails in its objectives but plays an important part in delaying Hodges' First Army during its advance to the Rhein. A supplementary parachute drop by a special detachment commanded by Freiherr von der Heydte also fails to secure its objective but causes a degree of American panic. Meanwhile, a new 8 Fallschirm 'Division', never more than a regiment in strength, begins forming at Köln-Wahn; it is commanded by Wadehn after Schimpf takes over 3 Fallschirm Division again.
1945	
January	**Eastern Front**: The two 'HG' divisions are encircled by Soviet forces around Heiligenbeil.
February	**Western Front**: 7 Fallschirm Division again delays the British XXX Corps, at Kappeln and during the Rhein crossings next month.
March	**Western Front**: 3 and 5 Fallschirm Divisions virtually annihilated west of the Rhein. The few survivors meet their end in the Ruhr Pocket, along with those from 2 Fallschirm Division. **Eastern Front:** Survivors of the two 'HG' divisions who manage to fight their way out are evacuated by sea to Denmark where they are taken under command by the Army's 'Großdeutschland' Panzerkorps.
April	**Italy**: 1 and 4 Fallschirm Divisions surrender near Bologna and Verona respectively. **Eastern Front**: Remnants of the 'HG' divisions surrender to Red Army troops in Saxony. A newly created so-called 9 Fallschirm 'Division' (Generalmajor Bruno Bräuer) is destroyed as the Soviets drive on Berlin, and the same fate befalls the equally embryonic 10 Fallschirm 'Division' (Generalmajor von Hofmann) in Czechoslovakia.
May	With the end of the war in Europe, 6 Fallschirm Division surrenders near Zutphen, 7 Fallschirm Division near Oldenburg and 8 Fallschirm 'Division' near Bremen.

RECRUITMENT AND ENLISTMENT

'Die Fahnen hoch, die Reihe dicht geschlossen!'
('The flags held high, the ranks stand tight together!')
First line of the song written in memorial to SA stormtrooper
Horst Wessel which became something of a Nazi anthem.

The date is 16 March 1939. Location, Koblenz, the attractive medieval township nestling on a spit at the confluence of the mighty rivers Rhein and Mosel. It lies in the heart of the Rheinland wine-growing region, with steep terraced slopes leading down to the banks of the rivers, all overlooked by the imposing Fort Constantine. In six years time it will be a smoke-blackened ruin after Allied bombing and the onslaught of General George Patton's US Third Army through its narrow cobbled streets. This early morning it is tranquil, although thick damp mist, undisturbed by the passage of the barges and lighters on the rivers, weakens the sun, chills the air and makes the real spring seem far away.

Wilhelm ('Willi') Schmidt's[3] eyes and mind ignore the familiar landscape as he trudges, greatcoat tightly buttoned against the cold, away from his parents' home towards the railway station at the foot of the steep bluff of the west bank of the Rhein. Just turned 19 a couple of months earlier, the new *Schütze* (Private) Schmidt is heading back to the barracks of the army infantry regiment based outside Wiesbaden to which he was assigned after conscription and basic training the previous year. Twelve months ago, he was still studying at school. Now, having passed his exams, he has become an insignificant molecule in the vast human army being recreated by Chancellor Adolf Hitler after the repudiation of the infamous Treaty of Versailles exactly five years earlier.

What met Schmidt in the draughty confines of the *Bahnhof* changed his life forever. The brightly coloured poster on the wall showed a swooping eagle alongside upraised flags. The forward momentum was self-evident, but what impressed Schmidt was the widespread, lethal talons of the swooping bird of prey. The image stayed in his mind after he boarded the train wending its way along the west bank of the Rhein towards Mainz. Oily smoke from the

German recruiting posters emphasised aggression with the swooping eagle denoting triumph. The caption on this early war example reads, 'Victory follows our banners'.

Newly trained Fallschirmjäger recruits, a couple of them still a little uncertain, march proudly beneath Nazi banners during a pre-war parade.

locomotive constantly billowed past the window, obscuring the river, the vineyards and the occasional picturesque castle perched high above. The scene was so familiar to Schmidt that there was more fascination in picking transitory images from the swirling smoke, and he kept imagining he saw the eagle descending.

Back in barracks, everything returned to normal as Schmidt and his pals exchanged largely fictitious accounts of the girls and bar brawls they'd enjoyed while on leave. Schmidt soon tired of the harmless banter, though, and went to his bunk to make sure his kit was ready for inspection later in the day. Opposite him, a lad he'd become friendly with during 'basic', Max Arent, was reading a pamphlet.

'What've you got there, Max?', Schmidt asked curiously. Arent tossed it to him.

'Recruiting crap, Willi. Picked it up on the train. The air force wants volunteers for parachute training. Sounds like a good way to commit suicide to me. Keep it with pleasure.'

The Luftwaffe eagle on the cover of the brochure, so much more flamboyant and lifelike than the army's more stylised version, struck an immediate chord and Schmidt began reading attentively. The more he thought about it, the more the idea appealed. Like most of his generation, he had never flown before, but he was curious. The prospect of being flown into battle comfortably, rather than marching through endless muddy fields, definitely had its merits. The only thing that gave him a twinge of doubt was the thought of actually jumping out of the plane and entrusting his life to an oversize umbrella. He decided to sleep on it, and tucked the pamphlet into his locker.

Young Schmidt would find out how quickly things could happen in the Wehrmacht, particularly if Reichsmarschall Hermann Göring, the inveterate empire-builder, had anything to do with them. Barely a week after having approached his company commander about volunteering for the Fallschirmtruppen, Schmidt found himself on a train again, heading northeast this time towards Berlin. That alone was exciting enough, because he had never visited the capital. Nor, as it happened, did he have a chance to do so now because he had to change trains to get to the town and airfield of Stendal, some 60 miles (90km) west of the city, which was the home of General Kurt Student's slowly growing 7 Flieger Division. At this time the division was only two battalions strong, but there was the normal degree of attrition and, in any case, Student had his eyes firmly focused on expansion, because everyone knew that a war was on its way.

Alighting at Stendal, Schmidt found himself part of a group of a dozen or so young men in a variety of uniforms, mostly air force but including a sprinkling from the army and one naval rating who looked decidedly out of place. They were driven by truck to the airfield, and then escorted by a corporal to the barracks hut they would share during the test programme that would determine their suitability as potential paratroopers. An exhausting mental and physical curriculum was spread over several days, and those who passed soon found out that the parachute school's own eight-week training programme was in some ways even harder. Before the trial by ordeal began, though, there was a thorough medical check. Firstly, anyone weighing over 85kg (13 stone) was told to lose weight quickly 'or else', because that was the maximum safe lifting capacity of the parachute then in use, the RZ 1. There was also an air experience flight in an ageing Dornier. For most, including Schmidt, this was an exhilarating first-time experience, but those who became dizzy or were sick were downgraded, because sickness causes dehydration and paratroops have to be fully fit and alert when they land. Fear of heights was also tested by making candidates jump into a tank of

In pre-war days, air travel was still a novelty that most people could not afford, so for many recruits in the Fallschirmtruppen boarding an obsolescent Dornier Do 23 was probably their first experience of flying.

water from a 15m (50ft) tower. Then came long cross-country runs and obstacle courses, both tackled against the clock and each other, individually or in teams; these tested natural aggression, will to succeed and the ability to work with others. The latter was particularly important because the volunteers came from many different parts of Germany, which in itself was a novel experience for most of them. Since conscription through the Wehrkreise was on a regional basis, all the men had shared at least some local affinity in their parent units. Now someone from Prussia, say, might find himself teamed up with a Bavarian, and each would have to learn to understand the other's dialect.

Other tests designed to highlight leadership qualities looked for initiative and imagination. Manual skills, such as field stripping and re-assembling weapons – again, against the clock – came under scrutiny too. There were also both written and oral exams on subjects as diverse as military law and National Socialist history and doctrine. The latter were not just to test candidates' knowledge, but also their literacy and fluency. Had Schmidt and the others volunteered for transfer to the 'Herman Göring' Regiment they would have found the entry requirements even tougher because they also involved investigation into each man's racial 'purity'. As it was, strange though it may seem, the Fallschirmjäger even accepted a tiny minority of men with Jewish ancestry[4].

The test, though, which caused many men to drop out voluntarily and others to be returned to their original units (RTU'd) as good soldiers but unsuitable paratrooper material, was the interview, which was conducted by Major Richard Heidrich in most cases. Major Heidrich was CO of II Fallschirmjäger Bataillon, and he was also at the time in charge of processing new intakes (*Kommandeur des neuaufzustellenden*).

Schmidt and the others had all discussed what they were going to say, but he had kept one answer carefully to himself. His friend Max Arent, back in Wiesbaden, had at some point asked the inevitable question, 'Why do you want to jump out of a perfectly good aeroplane?'. Lost for words at the time, Schmidt had thought of the answer which he now threw back at the Major. 'When the Luftwaffe builds a perfectly good aeroplane, Sir, I shan't need to.' Heidrich, who was looking for spirit amongst the recruits (and had an army, not air force background anyway), may even have smiled, but Schmidt's eyes were fixed on an imaginary point on the wall – as regulations demanded. Nevertheless, from that moment on he was 'in'. Later, there would be moments when he wondered why he had worked so hard to join the Fallschirmtruppen, but they lay far in the future. For the time being he was content with having been accepted, however provisionally, into the new elite force.

BELIEF AND BELONGING

'This new Reich will give its youth to no-one, but will itself take youth and give to youth its own education and its own upbringing.' (Dr Bernhard Rust)

Dr Rust, who had been sacked from his post as a provincial schoolmaster on the grounds of mental instability, frequently used words from Adolf Hitler's writings and speeches, which he turned into his own, as above. Hitler's rewards for Rust's dog-like devotion and fanaticism were to elevate him first to Prussian Minister of Science, Art and Education and then to

Although most Fallschirmtruppen only paid lip service to Nazism, there was a strong belief in the Führer. However, allegiance to the regiment and to the parachute corps were undoubtedly more important.

Reich Minister of Education in 1934. Dr Rust may have lacked talent, but he was a racist, and his prejudice was sufficient qualification for him to succeed politically and materially in the Germany of the mid-1930s. Unfortunately, Rust's warped mentality gradually pervaded almost every sphere of German life, including the world of the young Willi Schmidt and his peers while they were still at school.

German compulsory education for boys at the time extended until the age of 18, after which – following Hitler's rise to power – all young men had to join the *Wehrmacht* (Armed Forces, excluding the Waffen-SS) or do a term of service in the *Reicharbeitsdienst* (Reich Labour Service). The former was the more glamorous option which most elected for if given the choice. The resurgent tide of nationalism affected all Germans in the 1930s, and permeated the whole educational system. Schooling throughout Europe was, in any case, far more authoritarian than it is today and, particularly in Germany, the emphasis was firmly on duty and obedience to God and country, teachers, parents and policemen. The values of the education system, coupled with the nation's predominantly Lutheran faith, played straight into the hands of Hitler and his 'spin-doctors'.

Bernhard Rust was not alone amongst the deranged elements insidiously infiltrating themselves into the fabric of German society. The Protestant army *Geistliche* (Chaplain), Ludwig Müller, who had since 1932 effectively led the German Christians' Faith Movement and at Hitler's instigation became the first *Reichsbischof* (Reich Bishop), was also a significant figure. Müller and his followers, and there were many amongst the 45 million Protestants in Germany, firmly believed in religious freedom so long as it was not, to quote Hitler, 'a danger to the moral feelings of the German race'[5]. Religious freedom, of course, did not extend to Jews, but there was ample precedent for this. Martin Luther, the principal founder of Protestantism, had railed viciously against Jews (and gypsies) in the 16th century. His teachings also stressed the need for law and order, and obedience to the legally appointed authorities. Thus, even though one of Hitler's eventual secret aims was the abolition of Christianity and its replacement by a form of National Socialist paganism in line with the Aryan myth, the Protestant church became an ally alongside the schools in the indoctrination of a generation.

There were, of course, other voices in Germany at the time advocating something different to Rust's 'liquidation of the school as an institution of intellectual acrobatics' or Müller's Nazified Christianity[6]. Many church leaders, while initially welcoming Hitler's rise to power, found themselves gradually forced to stand against him. For their pains, most lost their jobs or worse. One such was Pastor Martin Niemöller, a First World War U-boat hero, who became their effective spokesman

The need for very close teamwork, whether packing a parachute or in the field, created a very strong camaraderie within the Fallschirmtruppen which was strengthened by the feeling of belonging to the elite.

and, as a result, lived out the war in a succession of concentration camps. Many schoolmasters suffered similar fates, but the majority (97 per cent) bowed with the wind and joined the Nazi *Lehrerbund* (a form of teachers' union) after a month-long ideological training course organised by the Party.

The infighting between the church, the schools and Nazi officialdom passed with little reaction from the man in the street, partly as a result of censorship but predominantly through simple apathy. The children and teenagers who would form the bulk of the German fighting forces in the Second World War knew little about it and cared even less, nor did they usually even realise its effects, because the changes in their upbringing were not, initially, cataclysmic.

Sport had always been stressed in German schools, and a renewed emphasis on physical fitness went unnoticed by most and was probably welcomed by the less academically minded. Similarly, few noticed that the teaching of history altered to give even more emphasis to Germanic achievements, particularly those in medieval times, and a more political slant favouring Nazi ideals. Religious education lessons became fewer and shorter, and emphasis was placed on eugenics in biology classes, in keeping with the ideal of the Master Race.

Even their opponents freely admitted that the Fallschirmtruppen fought fairly, without the viciousness encountered in some other formations, and treated prisoners well. In this now famous incident at Depienne, Tunisia, in November 1942, injured British paratroopers were saved from an Italian firing squad by a detachment from I Bataillon, 5 Fallschirm Regiment, commanded by Major Walter Koch; the same Koch who had earlier led his assault battalion to victory in Belgium in 1940 (see Plate D).

One change in the life of a teenager which did not pass unnoticed was membership of Baldur von Schirach's[7] *Hitler Jugend* (Hitler Youth). This movement had been started in 1926 as a junior section of the SA, the *Sturmabteilung* (Storm Troop), and, while borrowing much from the Boy Scouts, had a much more militaristic ethos. Wilhelm Schmidt and his contemporaries would have been members from at least the age of 15, since it was made compulsory in 1936 and parents who objected were heavily fined. Prior to 1936, the boys may have been voluntary members of the *Jungvolk* (Young Folk), which embraced 10- to 14-year-olds. Activities in both included running, swimming and other athletic pursuits, weekend cross-country camping hikes with map and compass, learning and practising semaphore, and arms drill, including range practice. In addition, classroom sessions emphasised Nazi doctrine and Party history, with endless readings from Hitler's *Mein Kampf* (My Struggle), and every boy had to learn the *Horst Wessel* song by heart. Older youths in the Hitler Jugend were given time off regular schooling for summer camps or attendance at Party rallies, and most wore their uniform and ceremonial dagger with immense pride. Those who did not, or otherwise showed they were unresponsive to the Nazi programme, ended up in the labour service when they reached the age of 18[8].

To have got as far as they did, Willi Schmidt and his classmates must have demonstrated attentiveness and instant obedience to orders, qualities which were both a great Germanic weakness in social terms and a strength in militaristic ones. But, if the regime seems doctrinal and harsh, the education systems in other European countries of the time differed little,

A well-defined sense of chivalry led the Fallschirmtruppen to treat wounded prisoners with consideration, as shown in this relaxed group on Crete in 1941.

Roughly 80 per cent of men in the Wehrmacht remained Christians despite Nazism, and many who were regular churchgoers in civilian life found great solace in the Sunday services conducted by the chaplain (*Geistliche*), who in this instance is an army officer. Note the armband with a violet cross, which was first issued to help protect clergy during the Russian campaign.

except in the political sense. Boys simply did what they were told, and if they erred they were punished physically at school and in most cases suffered even worse at home when their fathers discovered their transgression. Adolf Hitler and those who wormed their way into power on his bandwagon simply took the status quo and adapted it to their own ends.

The German nation as it existed in the 1930s and 1940s was a mere youth itself in the global context, having only been brought into political existence by Bismarck less than a century earlier. Nevertheless, this sense of achievement on the world stage was a strong motivation for the majority of people, helping to engender a sense of destiny in which belief and acknowledgement of belonging to something greater than oneself are paramount. The débâcle of the First World War, following two sweeping victories within living memory over Austria and France, and the ignominious, punitive terms of the Versailles Treaty had provoked enormous resentment, which Hitler and the Nazis used to their advantage during and after their rise to power. This same sense of resentment was passed on to young men of Wilhelm Schmidt's generation not only at school and in the Hitler Jugend, but also through parents and parish priests. What they saw in Adolf Hitler's Third Reich, therefore, was enormous forward progress on the home front and in Germany's relationships with other countries. Even people who harboured private doubts about much of National Socialist theory and doctrine recognised that achievements had been made, with regular pay packets now replacing the unemployment and inflation which had crippled the country such a short while ago. From their point of view the Fatherland was strong, prosperous and influential.

The end result was that most young men felt that what the State was doing was right. They also agreed with Hitler's decision to reintroduce conscription in 1935, and most concurred with the view that service in the armed forces was natural, that those who went into the labour corps or the 're-education centres' (which ended up as concentration camps) were weaklings who deserved it, and that *they* were going to do their best to make their parents and mentors proud.

Boot camp is much the same in any army, and after the discipline of school and in the Hitler Jugend, most recruits took to the early morning reveille, the spit and polish, the constant callisthenics and drill, the lectures and interminable route marches like ducks to the water. What changed after basic training, and even more so after being selected for an elite body of men such as the Fallschirmtruppen, was that recruits came across veterans from the First World War and the interwar *Reichswehr*, whose attitudes contradicted much of what the youngsters had been taught.

As a generalisation the Wehrmacht, and in particular the Heer, had an ambivalent attitude towards the Nazi Party. The majority of seasoned officers and NCOs may have applauded the growth in their numbers and influence, and the introduction of so much new technology, but they distrusted Hitler's motives. There were too many new concepts to assimilate, such as *Lebensraum* (Living room) and *Weltanschauung* (World view), and they were concerned where the Führer's ambitions might lead them. Thus, even while most welcomed the drift to war after the relatively uneventful takeovers of Austria and Czechoslovakia, they radiated an aura of world-weary cynicism that soon communicated itself to the new recruits in their midst. Young soldiers of a sensitive nature were left to decide who to believe. Fortunately, there was a practical solution, because a man's regiment soon became not only his family but also his *raison d'être*, even though he was obliged to continue to give lip service to National Socialism and had his oath to the Führer to live up to.

Some men remained fervent Nazis throughout the war, but the majority in the Fallschirmtruppen, judging from both diaries and postwar writings, rapidly lost their enthusiasm once the euphoria of the early victories had faded and campaigning became a simple struggle for survival. Unsurprisingly, this stimulated a return to earlier roots, and Sunday church meetings in the field, presided over by the regimental chaplain, were always well attended. Similarly, men learnt to catch up on sleep with their eyes open during the ongoing political lectures.

Two last factors were crucial in the moulding of a Fallschirmjäger. They were a sense of comradeship, and one of chivalry. Both came from the same source: a firm belief in oneself, from which stemmed a very strong 'do as you would be done by' outlook. Of course, on a battlefield this often devolves to 'kill or be killed', but not necessarily so, and opponents of the Fallschirmtruppen generally found them gracious rather than sullen in defeat and magnanimous in victory. The belief in 'self' (and, as already mentioned, in belonging to a greater 'self') came partly from earlier teaching by parents, school and church, and partly through the Fallschirmjäger selection procedure and rigorous training which cultivated the sense of belonging to an elite[9].

Camaraderie, always a significant force in any military unit and particularly so at the squad level, was vital to each and every Fallschirmjäger, not just because they helped each other pack their 'chutes but because they knew that after most drops they would be out on a limb, miles and hours or days from relief, and had to rely totally on each other. The sense of chivalry evolved from this, because comradeship was so intrinsic to the Fallschirmjäger ethos that they expected everyone, with the notable exception of partisans, to share it. Partisans are loathed by all regular troops in any war, largely because they melt back into the general populace after inflicting their damage. Hitler himself had also singled them out in his 'Ten Commandments' to the Fallschirmtruppen referred to earlier. 'Against an open foe,' he said, 'fight with chivalry, but extend no quarter to a guerrilla.' This admonition was remembered well on Crete and in Russia in particular, with the slightest suspects being summarily executed.

TRAINING

'Angeganen, Sie Affen! Ein impi von Zulus würde Sie abfangen und Sie vor Früstück esse!' (Come on, you apes! A Zulu impi could catch you and eat you for breakfast!) This unattributable quote was apparently uttered by an Obergefreiter leading a cross-country run in Bavaria. The trainee Fallschirmtruppen carried full kit while he just wore a singlet and trousers! The insult was deliberate, since despite their fighting qualities, Zulus had the wrong colour skin as far as the Nazis were concerned, and were classed as *Untermenschen* (sub-humans).

As mentioned earlier, if the new Fallschirmjäger hopefuls found the selection process tough, what followed was, to quote a genuine new recruit of the time[10], 'unbelievably hard, but basically fair. It passed quickly even if only because we were drilled so hard that we never got a moment to think.'

Most of Willi Schmidt's eight weeks at Stendal[11] were thus spent in strenuous physical exercise morning, noon and night, a toughening-up regime tailored to the Fallschirmjäger light infantry role. Speed was of the essence in virtually everything he and his comrades had to endure but, other than that, to begin with there seemed little difference between this new phase of training and what they had gone through in 'basic'. PE sessions and 'square bashing' occupied much of the day, alongside bayonet practice, unarmed combat sessions and weapons' instruction. Up to this point, most men had only really received tuition in using hand grenades and the Wehrmacht's standard Mauser Gew

ABOVE LEFT **After his first jump, with a 'chute packed by depot personnel, it became every jäger's responsibility to pack his own. In practice, it needed two people to fold it correctly, and each man was allowed to choose his most trusted friend to assist.**

ABOVE RIGHT **The correct posture for exiting a Ju 52 is demonstrated by former German heavyweight boxing champion Max Schmeling, an early volunteer for the Fallschirmtruppen. Although static lines can be seen to his left trailing out of the doorway as though a number of men have already jumped, this photo was obviously posed on the ground and he is not wearing his gauntlets. Note second pattern front-lacing boots.**

ABOVE LEFT **Suspended from the roof of an aircraft hangar, recruits learn the correct spread-eagled posture to adopt immediately after leaving the aircraft. This position kept the body stable in the air and lessened the shock when the 'chute opened.**

ABOVE RIGHT **An instructor shows how to throw the legs back and align the body forward just prior to landing. It can clearly be seen that there was no way the RZ1 or RZ16 parachutes could be steered using the twin attachment points behind the shoulders.**

98 rifle and Kar 98 carbine, conventional bolt-action weapons with five-round box magazines. Now they had to learn how to use a whole gamut of military hardware. Pistols, sub-machine-guns, machine-guns, mortars and mines were all introduced, and not just those of German manufacture. Recruits also practised using some of the foreign weapons they might encounter on a battlefield; such familiarity could save their lives, especially when dropped behind enemy lines.

Time was also taken up with both lectures on tactics and field exercises, beginning at the *Zug* or squad level and rising through section and company eventually to that of the whole battalion because, as in all armies, the battalion is the basic fighting unit. There were more obstacle courses to be overcome, but now these included replica fortifications with real barbed wire and dummy minefields. Fortunately, to most men's way of thinking, the political lectures dwindled, with more emphasis being given to bonding and team spirit, welding them together into a tight-knit, but flexible, unit. Despite this, many men began to wonder when they would get down to the real thing.

At last, however, the great day did arrive, and Schmidt's intake began the 16-day parachute course. Even before this, some of their training had been engineered to ease the transition from 'mudfoot' to 'sky warrior', because part of the physical exercise sessions had included, for example, executing a high jump on to a trampoline or somersaulting in the air over a couple of other recruits crouching on the ground. Such exercises would help the new Fallschirmjäger achieve the sort of 'boneless' fall that was essential for an injury-free landing. Additionally, the men had also received intensive instruction in parachute packing, a painstaking exercise that in most other countries was, and still is, entrusted to specialists, but which the German paras had to learn to do for themselves.

Before packing, the 'chutes were suspended from rails beneath the roofs of aircraft hangars to ensure they were dry and free of tears or wrinkles. Then they were laid lengthways on long trestle tables and carefully folded to a pattern which had, quite literally, evolved through trial and error. It took two men to do this, and each recruit chose his most trusted buddy to help because his life depended upon the quality of his colleague's work.

What followed was equally important because the design of the RZ 1 (Rückenpackung Zwangauslösung or 'rucksack packed to open'), and its successors, the RZ 16 and RZ 20, necessitated a special technique both for jumping from the aircraft (usually a Junkers Ju 52/3m) and for landing (see Plate B for further details). To achieve the necessary level of skill, the trainees used a mock-up door to practise the first and were then suspended from their harness by a wire from the hangar roof rail to perfect the second. It should be noted that, despite these precautions, there were numerous injuries and several fatalities caused through design faults in the RZ 1, which is inexplicable because the standard and reliable 'chute issued to Luftwaffe aircrew not only had lift webs to help control descent, but also featured a more sensible harness with a single central quick-release catch. Maybe it was thought that simple 'squaddies' would be incapable of mastering it?

All the parachutes issued to the Fallschirmtruppen were opened by means of static lines, not ripcords. This method permits drops from lower heights, resulting both in less time in the air when any paratrooper is particularly vulnerable to ground fire, and in tighter grouping once back on *terra firma*. The German parachute canopies themselves were 8.5m (28ft) in diameter and sewn from 28 gores (wedge-shaped pieces) of silk. They were packed in cloth bags. A thin cord attached the apex of the folded canopy to the mouth of the bag, and the bag was firmly attached to the 9m (29 $\frac{1}{2}$ft) static line. This length meant that the 'chute was already fully deployed by the time a man had fallen vertically some 25–30m (85–120ft), permitting drops from less than 100m (320ft). The bagged canopy with its carefully coiled-down shrouds was stowed in a stout canvas pack which clipped on to the harness webbing worn by the Fallschirmjäger. The static line was coiled under the flap on the back of the pack. To begin with this was on the right-hand side, but analysis of training mishaps caused it to be moved to the top.

Recruits had to complete six drops before they were entitled to wear the coveted *Fallschirmschützenabzeichen* (Parachutist's Badge). As Schmidt and his comrades board the aircraft for their first jump, they have already donned the bulky knee pads designed to prevent injury on landing, and each man has had his parachute harness and pack carefully checked by his instructor, who now serves as the *Absetzer* (despatcher). Once aboard, they clench the end of their static lines between their teeth to leave their hands free in case the aircraft runs into turbulence (or later, in battle, has to take evasive action to avoid enemy anti-aircraft fire or fighters). Once the aircraft has reached its designated height, the

OPPOSITE TOP **The great moment has arrived and an instructor checks his recruits' equipment before their first jump. Unusually, they are carrying their static lines right-handed, and not all have put on their outer knee protectors.**

OPPOSITE BOTTOM **Tension of the final moments is apparent from the pensive expressions on the men's faces. Sitting cramped knee-to-knee like this was extremely uncomfortable, and they must have almost welcomed the despatcher's order to 'Hook up'. It can just be seen that the 'chutes are the RZ16 model with static lines coiled on top of the packs.**

ABOVE **The moment of truth. The static line has just reached full stretch and the parachute pack of the lower figure, falling in the recommended spread-eagled posture, is just coming open while a second man vaults from the Ju 52's door.**

LEFT **In free fall, a body accelerates at 16 ft/sec^2 (4.88m/s^2) until terminal velocity is achieved, leaving an agonising few moments of uncertainty followed by an enormous feeling of relief and exhilaration as the 'chute cracks open with a resounding jerk. Then comes the landing, with the body meeting the ground at an average of 16 ft/sec, depending on a man's weight.**

despatcher orders the men to stand and hook their static lines to the cable running just above shoulder height along the length of the aircraft's fuselage. The first man in the 'stick' stands apprehensively in the doorway, braced as trained to launch himself cleanly out in the prescribed spread-eagled posture.

'Gehen Sie! Geh! Geh!' Shuffling forward, the men launch themselves into space, fractionally aware of other static lines trailing in the aircraft's slipstream and other canopies billowing into shape below them. The audible 'crack' and sudden gut-wrenching jerk as each man's own 'chute deploys safely brings immediate, almost unbelieving, relief, and then a huge surge of exhilaration to the paratrooper as he floats deceptively slowly towards the ground. Those still sufficiently aware to remember their training try awkwardly to twist themselves so that they are facing into the wind, to lessen the impact, because suddenly the ground, which moments ago seemed so far away, is now rushing up towards them. Their booted feet then their padded knees hit the ground and they roll, trying already to grab the shroud lines and deflate the 'chute which, in a moderate wind, could drag them across rocks or into water. Fortunately, each man has a special knife with which to cut

Fallschirmtruppen rapidly deploy behind an MG 34 team during an exercise, leaving their 'chutes billowing in the wind. Out of camera there must be a supply container from which they have retrieved their weapons.

ABOVE **The invasion of Norway, spring 1940. In this shot it can clearly be seen that the despatcher in the Ju 52 has thrown out the men's supply container first. Unfortunately, the RZ16 'chute could not be steered so the men could not aim to land near the container, resulting in wasted time – and often lives – before they could deploy.**

LEFT **In a battle zone, parachutes were abandoned for later collection. Here, however, Max Schmeling, a later hero of the battle for Crete, bundles his 'chute under his arm. In Russia, parachutes were sometimes cut up and recycled as snow camouflage capes.**

himself free if necessary. All of a sudden, it is over, and while some men simply brush themselves down others celebrate more enthusiastically.

Five more drops will follow, from different heights with varying wind speeds and including one in poor visibility, although strangely the Germans never seriously practised night drops, which was one of the reasons for the failure of Operation 'Stösser' during the Battle of the Bulge referred to elsewhere. Then comes the award of the silver and gilt qualifying badge, the handshakes from the instructors and the passing out parade through the streets of Stendal before each of the newly qualified Fallschirmjäger joins his battalion in 7 Flieger Division. The war, for the newly promoted Oberjäger (Private or Aircraftman First Class) Willi Schmidt, is now only three months away.

APPEARANCE AND EQUIPMENT

Fallschirmjäger clothing and equipment were designed to be practical, comfortable, and well suited to the battlefield of the 1940s. Unfortunately, the main distinguishing feature of a German para's apparel was his bright golden-yellow *Waffenfarbe* (arm of service colour) applied principally to collar patches and shoulder boards. Men of the 'Hermann Göring' Division(s) wore white. Both colours were wildly impractical on a battleground and were frequently removed or carefully muddied other than when an official photographer (*Kriegsberichter*) was around. Waffenfarbe apart, Willi Schmidt and his comrades wore

Jägers immaculately kitted out in first-pattern jump smocks and boots head towards a Ju 52 for a practice jump from a snow-covered airfield. This is clearly an early photograph, as the men do not wear the external knee pads which were introduced to help prevent injuries on landing. Both the smocks and boots were also changed radically after early battle experience in 1940.

standard Luftwaffe uniform and insignia with the exception of a few important items, most of which are illustrated or described in the captions to the photos and colour plates.

Starting at the top, the men's jump helmets (*Fallschirmhelme*) were originally cut-down Wehrmacht *Stalhelme* (steel helmets) with the brims removed. This was done partly to prevent the air flow of the initial descent from an aircraft lifting the helmet and half-strangling the men, and partly to eliminate the risk of the relatively sharp edges from possibly severing a shroud line. The helmets were initially painted Luftwaffe blue-grey and featured the national tricolour and air force eagle on either side (see Plate A). Battle experience soon caused them to be repainted green or, in North Africa and Italy, dull yellow, and the insignia disappeared. In winter, they were simply whitewashed, since this would scrub off easily in the spring. A variety of camouflage cloth helmet covers were issued as the war progressed. Men also made their own disruptive patterns using cut-down string vests or chicken wire, into which they inserted seasonal foliage (see Plate G). After 1941, with the virtual abolition of the Fallschirmtruppen as genuine airborne soldiers, an increasing number of men in the later-numbered divisions simply wore ordinary army helmets.

Other Fallschirmjäger headgear was standard Luftwaffe issue – sidecap (*Fliegermütze*), field cap with brim (*Einheitsmütze*) and both styles of officers' peaked cap (*Schirmütze*), in either blue-grey or tropical tan. For winter, especially in Russia, the men were issued with long woollen toques, tubular garments which fitted over their heads and necks rather like Balaclava helmets. A stylish peaked fur cap with ear flaps modelled on those issued to mountain troops also made an appearance, but it does not seem, from photographic evidence, to have been widely issued to the Fallschirmtruppen. One hat which did single out a Fallschirmjäger officer in the Afro-Mediterranean theatres was the so-called Meyer cap, a comfortable lightweight, loose, air-vented design with a detachable neck flap to protect against sunstroke (see Plate F).

Linen underwear, woollen socks, PE kit, fatigue overalls and white (parade), blue-grey or tropical tan shirts were standard for all ranks and no different from those issued to other Luftwaffe personnel. However, one individual item that became something of a Fallschirmjäger trademark in North Africa and later, was a brightly coloured neckerchief or silk scarf. Some regiments even adopted uniform colours: FJR 5's, for example, were dark blue with white polka dots.

Jackets and tunics were, again, standard Luftwaffe, either the stylish tapered-waist Flying Service Blouse (*Fliegerbluse*) or the four-

LEFT **A brief opportunity for an MG 42 section to take a cigarette break, as they shelter beside a solid stone wall in the ruins of Cassino. All wear second-pattern jump smocks in tan/brown camouflage, which is lighter in shade than the green splinter pattern more commonly seen. The officer or NCO with the binoculars has a mixture of canvas and leather MP 40 pouches on his belt.**

BELOW **German and Italian paratroopers in informal discussion. The man in the centre is rather slovenly dressed with a roll-neck pullover under his unbelted *Fliegerbluse*, while the jäger on the left still retains a plain grey/green first-pattern jump smock. Italian camouflage material was also quite extensively used by the Fallschirmtruppen.**

pocket Service Tunic (*Tuchrock*) (see Plate E); only the latter appears from photographs to have been issued in tropical tan material.

Jackets were belted at the waist and all ranks normally wore a holstered sidearm (see Plate C). Over the jacket, the Fallschirmtruppen wore the jump smock (*Fallschirmkittel*), a practical garment made of heavy duck cotton or, later, herringbone weave, which was designed to prevent clothing or equipment getting snagged in the aircraft or entangled in the parachute shroud lines at the moment of opening. The first pattern smock (see Plates A and D) was not, however, easy to put on or take off, because it had short integral legs. The jäger had to step into the legs, pull the garment up to his shoulders and then struggle into the sleeves before buttoning up the front. On landing, after freeing himself from the parachute harness (see Plate B), the jäger then had to pull the smock down to his waist in order to undo his equipment belt and buckle it back on outside the smock. To add insult to injury, he had to take the smock

RIGHT TOP **A squad of *Fallschirm-Pioniere* (parachute engineers) bring Teller mines up to the front. The Modell 42 and 43 both contained 5.2kg (11.5lb) of Cyclonite/TNT with the ability to penetrate just under an inch (actually 24mm) of armour, blow off tank tracks and wheels and inflict serious injuries to any accompanying infantry. The man in the background has his entrenching spade handily tucked in his belt, while the one in the foreground has stick grenades tucked in the hip pockets of his jump smock.**

RIGHT BOTTOM **Dress standards inevitably deteriorated on campaign, as this MG 42 section admirably demonstrate. The weapon actually has a drum magazine fitted but the men are all carrying loose 50-round belts or boxes of 7.92mm ammunition, and have netting loosely covering their helmets into which to tuck foliage.**

Group of jägers in the Normandy *bocage* wearing a mixture of jump helmets and ordinary *Stalhelme*. The man in the foreground has a Kar 98 slung across his back and what appears to be a Gew 43 with grenade launcher cup under his arm.

off again, or at least pull it down to his knees, in order to relieve himself. The first pattern smocks differed slightly from one another in the number of pockets they had (see Plate D), and were produced in either pale green or grey.

Most men involved in the 1940 campaigns wore the first pattern smock even though by this time the second had emerged. The later model was of a more practical design that omitted the legs of the first pattern smock, and which buttoned all down the front. On a jump, the lower half buttoned round the upper legs to recreate the earlier legs and prevent the smock billowing up as the jäger fell. The smock also had two large chest and thigh pockets and was manufactured in a green or tan/brown splinter camouflage pattern (see Plate F). A later variant of this garment, although not designated 'third pattern', was produced in more subtle brownish water camouflage after the Crete operation, and combat trousers were also introduced in this material (see Plate G).

Finally, after 1942, with the virtual abolition of the paratroop mission, an increasing number of Fallschirmtruppen (especially in the higher numbered divisions) were issued with the same single-breasted combat jacket (*Kampfjacke*), made of a rayon/cotton mix in splinter camouflage, as that issued to the Luftwaffe field divisions (see Plate G). Reports of a jump smock being produced in tropical tan are unsubstantiated, although some officers may have had these tailored privately. Other smocks were, however, sewn from Italian camouflage material after the armistice in 1943. The only insignia worn on any smocks or combat jackets (except on parade, when decorations were permitted) were the Luftwaffe breast eagle and cloth rank patches on the sleeves. Other special clothing issued after the first disastrous winter in Russia included at least two patterns of quilted jacket and trousers in reversible white/mouse grey colours (see Plate E). These garments were designed to give the Fallschirmtruppen more freedom of movement and action in extreme weather conditions than the standard double-breasted greatcoat (*Mantel*), but they were never available in sufficient quantity. It should be noted that the greatcoat was never worn over the jump smock.

For most of the war the Fallschirmtruppen wore combat trousers (*Hosen*) in a slightly darker grey-green material than their smocks. Hosen were relatively loose fitting for comfort and ease of movement, and fastened at the ankles with tapes. They had two side and two hip pockets plus a small fob pocket under the waistband, and could be held

JÄGER, 1940
(see plate commentary for full details)

A

PARACHUTE JUMPING AND EQUIPMENT
(see plate commentary for full details)

1

2

3

4

B

SIDEARMS AND PERSONAL WEAPONS (see plate commentary for full details)

1

1a

1b

1c

1d

1e

1f

A

B

2

3

4

5

6

7

8

8a

9

10

VOR GEBRAUCH
SPRENGKAPSEL
EINSETZEN

P38

C

STURMGRUPPE 'GRANIT', EBEN EMAEL, 10 MAY 1940

D

E

KEEPING OUT THE COLD: BUNKER LIFE, RUSSIA 1942

ON CAMPAIGN IN THE APENNINE FOOTHILLS; ITALY 1943

F

1

1a

1b

4a

2

3

4

G

up with either braces (suspenders) or a belt, depending upon personal preference. Uniquely, on the outside of each knee there was a vent through which the jäger could withdraw the rectangular kapok filled canvas pads which were worn to protect the knees in the heavy frontal fall dictated by the absurd parachute design (see Plate B). The system, however, proved ineffective, so external pads were also later strapped on (see Plate A). Both sets of pads were quickly discarded after landing to give more freedom of movement.

A final distinction of the Fallschirmjäger's trousers was the small pocket fastened with plastic press studs on the right thigh, and which carried the so-called 'gravity knife' (see Plate C). Unlike an ordinary clasp knife, which requires two hands to open, the Fallschirmjäger knife had a weighted blade that slid free automatically as it was taken out of the pocket, and was locked in place by a simple thumb catch. It was specially designed to allow a paratrooper, who already had one hand fully occupied trying to gather in his billowing 'chute, to cut the shroud lines and quickly free himself. The knife could, of course, also be used in combat or for eating. In North Africa and elsewhere the Fallschirmtruppen were issued with tropical trousers or shorts in a comfortable lightweight but hard-wearing cotton. The trousers (see Plate F) were particularly baggy to increase air flow and prevent chafing, and had both two generous hip pockets and a map pocket on the left thigh.

A Fallschirmjäger's uniform was also distinguished by the gauntlets (*Handschuhe*) and jump boots (*Fallschirmschnürschuhe*) (see Plate A). The soft black leather gloves, elasticated at wrist and cuff, were designed to keep the jäger's hands warm both inside the unheated cabin of the Ju 52/3m transport aircraft and during the drop itself. They were also sufficiently supple to be worn in combat. The boots, made of black

Fallschirmtruppen man an 8.8cm Flak 18/36 in Normandy. The '88' in its various guises was the gun Allied tank crews feared most. The man in the centre wears the third pattern jump smock and padded trousers in water-pattern camouflage.

RIGHT A Fallschirmjäger ski patrol in Russia wearing a mixture of Luftwaffe and Gebirgsjäger clothing, including white ski suits. The two men on the left have the very practical Luftwaffe version of the mountain troops' fur-lined ski caps (*Bergmütze*).

BELOW With two pistols strapped to his belt and an MP 40 in his right hand, the foreground jäger also carries a *Haft-Holladung* 3kg (6.6lb) magnetic hollow-charge anti-tank mine. These were predominantly used in close-quarters fighting in towns, but special squads of almost suicidal volunteers also formed tank hunter (*Panzerjäger*) teams under a variety of conditions.

leather with cleated rubber soles for grip, were originally laced at the side under the mistaken belief that this would offer extra ankle support. The second pattern had standard frontal lacing. Canvas ankle gaiters could be worn with either. However, on parade and as the war dragged on, in the field too, the Fallschirmtruppen wore the standard calf-length Wehrmacht jackboots (*Marchstiefeln*).

Field equipment for the individual Fallschirmjäger was, as is noted in the plate captions, more or less the same as that issued to army and Luftwaffe field divisions, although in the early days the paratrooper was issued with a soft canvas carrying bag for his gasmask instead of the rigid cylindrical metal one, which could have caused injury during a drop. A special ammunition bandolier was also developed for the Fallschirmtruppen (see Plates D and E). Personal weapons were identical to everyone else's, with the exception of the specially designed *Fallschirmgewehr* 42 assault rifle (FG 42) (see Plate G). There was also a higher allocation of other automatic weapons, including the MP 40 and MG 34/42, and pockets or waistbelts bulged with grenades. The Fallschirmtruppen also had a cut-down lightweight version of the army's standard 8.8cm mortar, the *kurzer* (short) *Granatwerfer* 42.

Because of the limitations on what a jäger could carry on his person during a drop, the Germans developed a rigid lightweight container to protect weapons and ammunition on their descent (see Plate B). Rifles and bandoliers, sub-machine-guns and ammunition pouches, machine-guns, mortars and ammunition boxes were all stowed away in these devices. Other containers, clearly marked with red crosses, carried medical and surgical equipment. Because the Fallschirmtruppen needed to get at their weapons very quickly once on the ground, the supply containers were normally thrown out of the aircraft before the first man jumped, giving him an aiming point. However, not all weapons went in the containers and, despite the risks, about one man in four dropped on Crete carried an MP 40 tucked under his parachute harness or strapped to his outer thigh. Similarly, during demonstration jumps for the 'brass' at Stendal, carbines were carried very unsafely in the hands. Nevertheless, despite the clumsiness of the German container system, the Fallschirmtruppen never imitated the British practice of stowing weapons and other equipment in a kitbag which could be dangled on a rope below each man, but given the impracticality of the RZ parachutes, this might have posed an unacceptable hazard.

At a higher level, anti-tank weaponry was important, and here magnetic mines and the *Panzerfaust* (armoured fist) and RPzB 54 came into their own, replacing the little sPzB 41 (see Plates F and G). Recoilless guns such as the 7.5cm and 10.5cm IG 40s and 42s (*Infanteriegeschütze* or infantry guns), although outside this book's remit, were also used because they were light in weight and could be dropped by parachute clusters or landed in gliders. Their big drawback in combat was that the backblast from the counter-propellant, which prevented recoil, was both a hazard to friendly troops and a give-away to the enemy, and from photographic evidence most seem to have been used just in training exercises or for the benefit of the Kriegsberichter.

EVERYDAY LIFE

With Schmidt now assigned to a battalion, the hectic pace of the past few weeks began to slacken. He was even given a few days' leave, during which he was able go home to Koblenz, proudly wearing his new Luftwaffe Fliegermütze and Fliegerbluse, the latter with the Parachutist's Badge pinned prominently on his chest. For the rest of the

Like most soldiers, the principal subject of a Fallschirmjäger's conversation when not in action was women, and this officer on leave has apparently struck lucky. His rank remains a mystery since, although his collar patches have the oakleaf worn by a Hauptmann, Oberleutnant or Leutnant, there are no wings to specify which.

time, life in barracks passed uneventfully. Callisthenics and drill continued, of course. Germany was preparing for war, and it was essential that the country's men be kept honed physically and mentally. Both field exercises and lectures now concentrated on small unit tactics, alongside practical exercises in first aid and constant weapons practice so that, in the end, the men could clear blockages or even strip and re-assemble their rifles and sub-machine-guns blindfolded. There were further practice parachute jumps and training flights in the DFS 230 glider. Preparations even extended to irregularly spaced surprise alerts in the middle of the night. There were also, inevitably, household chores to be done – kit and weapons cleaned, for example, and barracks swept, dusted and polished, while each man had to take his turn on the sentry duty roster and unfortunate transgressors endured punishment fatigues.

There was, however, time for leisure, for listening to the radio, playing records, reading books, writing letters or simply indulging in every soldier's favourite pastime of catching up on sleep. Sport was popular too, and the warm summer of 1939 offered plenty of opportunities for going swimming or playing football. In the evenings the men could visit the camp cinema, play cards or chess or, on privileged occasions, take a trip into Stendal itself to have a drink or a meal and socialise away from the canteen for a change.

The invasion of Poland on 1 September followed by the French and British declarations of war altered little for the majority of the Fallschirmtruppen, and like most of the rest of Europe they yawned their way through the months of the 'phony war' while their superiors planned how they were to be deployed in the assaults on Denmark, Norway, Belgium and Holland. The Fallschirmtruppen's part in these campaigns was violent but mercifully short-lived. Life returned to normal for the best part of a year, although there was a new air of confidence amongst the men and a number now had Iron Crosses or Wound Badges to display. Then came the attacks on Greece and Crete which were a bloodletting and a lesson but, again, the campaigns were so fast and furious that there was no time to think about normal life: there was a job to be done.

The first real experience of sustained campaign life came when 7 Flieger Division was posted to Russia in September. Here, on the Leningrad front, the Fallschirmtruppen found themselves facing a very different foe, a ruthless, remorseless enemy and a no-holds-barred battlefield. Now, the men learned to live in trenches and bunkers with no civilised amenities, no friendly bars, restaurants or cinemas and usually just a blanket over a straw-filled palliasse for a bed. Under these conditions the weather, in everyday life just part of the background, began to consume much of the men's conversation. When it rained the Luftwaffe, which at this time enjoyed

The Germans allowed proxy marriages for soldiers serving abroad and here, in the Western Desert, Oberst Bernhard Ramcke looks on paternally as a member of his brigade signs the documents marrying him to a girl back home.

ABOVE **Apart from women, drink is another preoccupation with most soldiers. This lucky Feldwebel (Sergeant) has managed to liberate a bottle of wine or beer; the lettering on the label is indistinct.**

RIGHT **Lunchtime for a pair of 2cm Flak gunners. Note both their helmets have camouflage covers to match their second pattern jump smocks.**

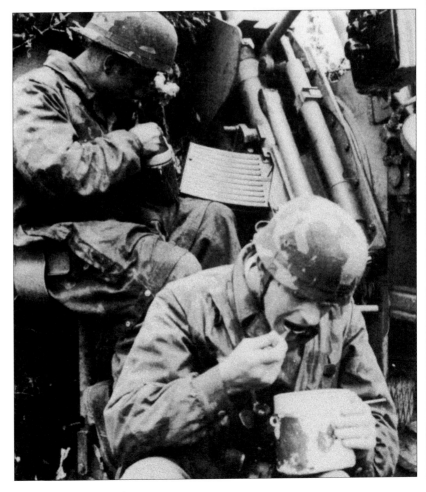

aerial supremacy, was unable to support attacks or help break up Soviet counter-attacks. There was also the impossible task of trying to stay dry or get clothes dried. Later, with the beginning of the autumn freeze, there was both the appalling cold to contend with and the swirling snowstorms that could hide an enemy attack until their bayonets were visible. Body lice were a constant irritation. To top it all there was the incessant shellfire from the Russian batteries that circled Leningrad, although most men, through sheer exhaustion, even learned to sleep through this noise. Food, most of the time, was not a hardship this early in the war, because the mobile field kitchens were still able to supply at least one hot meal a day even if it was not *haute cuisine*.

In December the bulk of 7 Flieger Division was relieved in the line and the survivors, shaken but not yet demoralised by their first taste of total war, found themselves back in Stendal. For some, however, it was a short-lived respite because they discovered themselves drafted into a new brigade intended to spearhead an airborne assault on Malta. When this was called off, the men were enplaned for North Africa to join Rommel. Here, 'everyday life' assumed another new meaning. The adversaries now were the heat by day and the unexpected chill at night, the constant sand, dust and grit which invaded every pore of the skin and made keeping weapons clean an even more essential chore, and the flies, the nauseating swarms of flies everywhere. Food, or the lack of it, also became a real preoccupation, as unlike in other theatres of war, it was not possible to forage in the desert to supplement the normal ration issue, although the occasional scrawny goat did make its way into the stewpot. The

ABOVE **Fresh milk today for a section of jägers billeted on a Normandy farm in 1944. Even after D-Day, daily life had to continue.**

OPPOSITE TOP **Even when off-duty, it was normal to keep a weapon handy in enemy territory, and the city of Rome became, effectively, just that after the Italian capitulation. This does not seem to be stopping these three men from enjoying the sights of the Eternal City.**

OPPOSITE BOTTOM **Probably in search of a bar, an off-duty squad in a French town exchange banter with a pair of comrades standing on sentry duty.**

RIGHT **Chores are part of everyday life for all soldiers, and here two jägers lead a pack mule laden with supplies to an outpost on an Italian hillside.**

tinned Italian sausages, which were provided along with each man's daily loaf of bread (freshly cooked in mobile field bakeries), pot of margarine and mug of *ersatz* (replacement) coffee, tasted disgusting and were virtually indigestible. Fresh fruit and vegetables were scarce and diarrhoea, dysentery and scurvy soon struck, while the medics kept a watchful eye for any sign of the dreaded typhus. The only consolation in this roll-call of misery was the occasional bottle of Italian wine.

Those Fallschirmtruppen who survived their African safari and later found themselves in Italy believed, initially, that they had drawn a 'cushy billet'. The food was now wholesome and plentiful, there was plenty of wine and, away from the front line, there was the splendid scenery, the beautiful *signorinas* and the magnificent city sights to enjoy. But in Italy there was also the growing awareness that the Third Reich was now on the defensive even though the subject was rarely discussed, except with the most trusted friends. However, Willi Schmidt and his comrades knew the end was in sight, despite Hitler's promises of 'wonder weapons', when they were ordered to abandon the Gustav Line and Rome fell. Two days later came the news of the Allied landings in Normandy, but there would be many more miles to trudge and battles to fight before they could rest.

The first taste of real action for the Fallschirmjäger in their true role came in Denmark and Norway in April 1940 and was only a partial success due to weather and unexpected resistance. It should, however, have warned the rest of Europe to expect more of the same.

EXPERIENCE OF BATTLE

'I heard a noise. I turned to the right and there I saw a black soldier in front of me. If I remember correctly, he laughed, but in a situation like this you remember your training – he who shoots first lives longer.'

Feldwebel Willi Renner (not Schmidt, this is a true account although some is paraphrased) was a member of FJR 6 – Friedrich Freiherr von der Heydte's old command – dug in near Obermarch on the Belgian-German border on Christmas Day 1944, at the height of the Ardennes offensive. Unknown to the Sergeant, his former CO, having valiantly tried to secure his objective during Operation 'Stösser', had been captured with a broken arm three days earlier. Renner continues: 'I had a machine-pistol and I was about to shoot, but because of the cold and the poor conditions of the last few days, I was only able to get one shot off. Anyway, he disappeared back in the hedge.

'I was checking my company's emplacements and eventually I got back to the last position, which was a machine-gun post with its guns pointed at the valley where the Americans were on the other side. I was a bit puzzled, everything was so quiet, then suddenly someone shouted at me, "Hey, What the hell are you doing? You'll be blasted out of sight!". Shots rang out and I dived for cover, but my legs were sticking out. I felt a sudden "thump". It's a really strange feeling – a dull thud as if someone has just hit you with a heavy club. I scrambled in panic into the machine-gun hole and my mates tore up some pieces of bed sheets. They wrapped them round my legs as an emergency dressing. I lay there for an hour, but after a while the pain was too much. I decided to make a "run" for it. Eventually I managed to scramble out on my stomach. A few seconds passed then I heard one of the Americans, who obviously spoke German, shout "komm rüber" [Come over]. I could have given myself up, but there's always the possibility that you are accused of deserting to the other side. I thought there was no way I could let that happen. I threw myself aside, crawled on my elbows for a while, then flung myself into the bush. There was a lot of firing but I managed to get back to my comrades. One of them hauled me across a turnip field and did his knee in, but we carried on and finally reached the company command post where there was a doctor.'

War, of course, is never glamorous. It's nasty, brutal, dirty and filled with pain, unendurable noise, confusion, dust, smoke, debris and blood. Von der Heydte, whose FJR 6 was the only Fallschirmjäger unit in the front line on D-Day back in June 1944, certainly encountered confusion behind 'Utah' beach. 'On the first day I received no orders. I was my own boss. The only contact was through the French phone network. [We] were forbidden to use this because of the French Resistance sabotaging the lines. I came across an old church tower in St Côme du Mont, got hold of the key, and went up there to take a look out over the coast. The forces we had were not in a position to offer a vigorous resistance. At every mile along the coast was a bunker and, of the three I could see, only one was firing at the Americans. I felt my Fallschirmtruppen were very vulnerable. I made a

The real vindication of the Fallschirmjäger theory came during the invasions of Belgium and Holland. In this rare photograph taken during the fighting, a flamethrower team is seen in action against one of the gun positions at Eben Emael.

LEFT **The sternest test for the Fallschirmtruppen was on Crete. Faulty intelligence conspired with the rugged terrain, strong Allied resistance in several places, lack of naval support, the activities of Cretan partisans and a variety of other factors to create insupportable casualties and write *finis* to any further large-scale paratroop operations.**

BELOW **After Crete, the next endurance tests for the Fallschirmtruppen came in two vastly different climes: North Africa and northern Russia. In this photo, the officer wearing a 'Meyer' cap and dust goggles appears from his own and his men's relaxed attitude to be pointing out the sights rather than the enemy, but the fighting itself was very hard.**

In blizzard conditions with near zero visibility, the Fallschirmjäger crew of a 5cm PaK 38 peer out as they wait for the next Soviet tank to materialise.

detour back to my command post and came across a German artillery battery which had been totally deserted. This was the second line of defence! When I finally contacted Marcks [Generalleutnant Erich Marcks, CO of LXXXIV Korps] I told him I had to try to defend the line north of St Côme du Mont. But then I had to leave because someone, I don't know who, had given the order to the engineers to blow up all the bridges [over the River Douve]. All the forces north of Carentan had been given the order to withdraw, because "we" were afraid "we" would be surrounded. I said it's nonsense [but] we had to do it. The water was up to our chests and we had all our heavy guns with us. Two of my soldiers drowned.'

Earlier in the war, things had at times been slightly easier for the Fallschirmtruppen. The then Oberleutnant (1st Lieutenant) Rudolf Witzig, who led Sturmgruppe 'Granit' in the assault on Eben Emael once he secured a second tow for his glider (see Plate D), says: 'Our final task was to blow in the fortified entrances and press the attack into the depths of the fortress, holding all captured positions until relief arrived. During some hours of moderate fighting, we managed to reconnoitre the entrances and we penetrated the installations already captured, but then the Belgian artillery started to shell our positions and their infantry attacked us repeatedly over the north-western slope, which was covered with dense undergrowth. Later we learned from Belgian sources that this was no counter-attack, but merely reconnoitring advances. That night was uneventful. After the hard fighting during the day, the detachment lay, exhausted and parched, under scattered fire. Every burst might have signalled the beginning of the counter-attack we feared, and our nerves were tense. About 07:00 hours [on 11 May] the advance section of 51 Pionier Bataillon at last arrived at the fortification. We retired after burying our dead and handing over our prisoners.'

Both the capture of Eben Emael and that of Crete a year later were milestones in the justified creation of the Fallschirmjäger legend, but every victory in war comes at a price. Oberfeldwebel (Sergeant-Major or Flight Sergeant) Walter Wachter was the pilot of a DFS 230 during the invasion of Crete. He recalls that, 'A huge red cloud of dust hung over the airfield. Within 15 minutes my *Kette* [flight of three aircraft] was all

set to go with a crew of eight Fallschirmtruppen each. The Ju 52s rolled forward. The overloaded glider rumbled along clumsily behind the towing aircraft and wouldn't leave the ground. Slowly we were pulled into the air.

'Everyone was lost in his own thoughts. The open sea lay before us. We had now reached our unhooking height. It was a peaceful flight in the first light of dawn. Suddenly the towing aircraft to the right of us drew ahead, trailing a rope but no glider. We now had 20 men – too few. We could see a lot of mushroom-shaped smoke clouds – the bombers were at work, preparing the ground. At intervals I could make out the lie of the land. A few bushes and trees were blocking the landing area. We were soon close to the landing point but too high. We had to move very swiftly – we couldn't present a target for the Flak. Everything was happening so fast now. Smash! Into a bush. The left wing struck a tree and broke off. The glider rocked and stayed still. The crew were unscathed – we all climbed out.'

Wachter was lucky, although later in the day he was wounded by smallarms fire. Perhaps an even more harrowing experience befell 19-year-old Jäger (Private) Karl Eisenfeller from Nr. 2 Kompanie of FJR 3 who, like many of his comrades, had been parachuted into a landing a considerable distance from the designated point. His first problem was how to rejoin his unit so, abandoning even his helmet in the ferocious heat but not the pistol which was his only weapon, he approached a cluster of houses. His next sight was two dead jägers lying in a pool of blood, then a Cretan woman doing her washing, who screamed loudly. Bypassing her house, he entered the village, where a number of young men were lounging around. Trying to conceal his fear,

ABOVE **After Russia, many men welcomed being posted to Sicily and Italy, but the battles themselves were equally hard-fought, and this PaK 38 crew appear to have their hands full.**

OPPOSITE TOP **The hardest fighting of all in Italy was for the town and monastery of Cassino. Here, a shell or bomb explosion shakes the cameraman's hands as he records a machine-gun crew peering through binoculars for their next target.**

OPPOSITE BOTTOM **The end of the war, and defeat for Hitler's Third Reich, are less than a year away but, despite their wounds, the eyes of these Fallschirmtruppen in Normandy show a flash of resigned humour.**

Eisenfeller approached them and begged a drink of water before trudging on, spine crawling in expectation of a bullet in his back. 'Fortunately,' he said after finally rejoining his unit despite running a more serious gauntlet of fire from a British patrol, 'they only shot when I was quite a way down the road, and they missed!'

The last word on Crete goes to Hauptmann Gerhard Schirmer from II/FJR 2 who jumped at Heraklion. 'It was a hard fight, but we knew whenever you fought against the English, it was a fair fight. We were able to send over envoys and agree on a ceasefire, say, of an hour, so that both sides could retrieve their wounded.' Like Wachter, Eisenfeller and Schirmer also survived the war – as did Oberjäger Robert Frettlohr who settled in Yorkshire, England, at the end of hostilities. He was captured by Polish troops in the ruins of Monte Cassino monastery. At the time he was serving with the engineer company of FJR 4.

'On April 1 I was posted to Rocco Janula [Castle Hill] and I was up there until the order came to retreat. They were shelling us all the time as we went up. As a young man of 20 years old, it was impossible to know what you felt. They kept telling you that you had to fight for your country. Forget it. You fight for self-survival. If anyone gets killed, you say, "It's not me". Anyone who says they weren't scared is lying – you were scared, all the time.

'After we'd rested, we waited to time the shells – one, two – then two of us would take off – always by twos. Then it was my turn. There was a flash close by and – I don't know. I passed out. When I woke up I crawled up to the monastery and got to the first aid post, which was where St Benedict was buried. The doctor put a bandage round my leg and said, "That's it, you're not going back". If there had been a road and I'd had a stick, I would have tried to get back, but there was no road, only rock.' Left behind with other wounded who could not walk, he was treated kindly by his captors, who sent him to an aid station and thence into captivity.

The eastern front was a different world, and I would like to end with the following valediction from Leutnant Friedrich Buschele, attached to Kampfgruppe 'Sturm', who was killed by Russian partisans in the winter of 1942 but whose diary survived. 'Everywhere the forests and marshes are haunted by the ghosts of the avengers. They would attack us unexpectedly, as if rising from under the earth. They cut us up to disappear like devils into the nether regions. The avengers pursue us everywhere. You are never safe from them. Damnation! I never experienced anything like it anywhere during the war. I cannot fight the sceptres of the forest. While I am making this entry, I look with anxiety at the setting sun. It is best not to think about it.'

What of our 'Willi Schmidt'? Did he survive? Maybe one day somebody will write a book about him …

The end of a long, hard road for many of the Fallschirmtruppen came in the Ardennes at Christmas 1944, when a deranged Führer ordered them into an abortive new offensive which came to be centred around the crossroads town of Bastogne.

NOTES

1 This was deliberately misleading to potential enemy intelligence services since there were no numbers 1–6.

2 A prime example of this occurred during the Battle of the Bulge in December 1944, when the simple knowledge that a German parachute force of then unknown size had been dropped behind American lines tied down a large number of men hunting for them. These men could more usefully have been employed further south helping to blunt the Panzer spearheads.

3 This is not a work of fiction. The persona of Willi Schmidt has simply been introduced as a device in an attempt to give the Fallschirmjäger experience more immediacy. Koblenz has been chosen as a starting point merely because the author has spent more weeks exploring its environs than any other part of Germany. Wiesbaden, which today enjoys a flourishing wargames club, was in the 1930s and 1940s the headquarters of *Wehrkreis* (Military District) XII. The Wehrkreise were responsible for recruitment and training within their own regional catchment areas and, later, for rebuilding combat-shattered divisions.

4 Evidence for this comes from Friedrich Freiherr von der Heydte, a Fallschirmjäger icon who postwar became a Fellow of the Carnegie Endowment for International Peace. In his fine book *Dædalus Returned* (Hutchinson, 1958), he recalls that, 'I had two Jews in my regiment [FJR 6]. Both used false names. One was the nephew of Albert Schweitzer and the other was the son of a German aristocrat whose mother was Jewish.'

5 Hitler himself had been brought up as a Roman Catholic and established an uneasy alliance with the Vatican by agreeing, through the Concordat of July 1933, not to interfere with the religious freedom of German Catholics so long as their priests did not get involved in politics.

6 It can be noted with some satisfaction that both Müller and Rust committed suicide rather than face imprisonment after the war.

7 Sentenced to 20 years' imprisonment after the first Nürnberg Trials.

8 There was always an element of resistance to the Hitler Youth movement, and a special section was even created in the RSHA (*Reichsicherheitshauptamt*, or Main Office of Reich Security) to investigate and deal with juvenile malcontents. 'Crimes' for which many were imprisoned or hanged included distributing anti-Nazi literature or even just listening to the BBC.

9 An anomaly here is that all these characteristics could be said to have been shared by the early Waffen-SS formations, whose men certainly shared comradeship amongst themselves but only rarely showed it to 'outsiders'.

10 Martin Pöppel, author of *Heaven and Hell: The War Diary of a German Paratrooper* (Spellmount, 1988).

11 During the war, centralised parachute training was abandoned and relegated to regimental training schools. However, shortages of aircraft and fuel meant that few men in the higher-numbered Fallschirmjäger divisions received any jump training. The CO of 4 Fallschirm Division, Generalmajor Heinrich Trettner, for example, was not entitled to wear the Parachutist's Badge.

SELECT BIBLIOGRAPHY

Ailsby, Chris, *Sky Warriors: German Paratroopers in Action 1939–45*, Spellmount, 2000

Davis, Brian L., *German Parachute Forces 1935–45*, Arms & Armour Press, 1974

Gregory, Barry, and Batchelor, John, *Airborne Warfare 1918–1945*, Phoebus, 1979

Hetherington, John, *Air-borne Invasion: The story of the battle of Crete*, Angus & Robertson, 1944

Heydte, Friedrich Freiherr von der, *Daedalus Returned*, Hutchinson, 1958

Kühn, Volkmar, *Deutsche Fallschirmjäger im Zweiten Weltkrieg* 5th edn, Motorbuch Verlag, 1985

Lucas, James, *Screaming Eagles: German Airborne Forces in World War Two*, Arms & Armour Press, 1988

Pöppel, Martin, *Heaven and Hell: The War Diary of a German Paratrooper*, Spellmount, 1988

Quarrie, Bruce, *Airborne Assault*, Patrick Stephens, 1991; *Fallschirmpanzerdivision 'Hermann Göring'*, Osprey, 1978; Men-at-Arms 139 *German Airborne Troops 1939–45*, Osprey, 1983

Weeks, J., *Airborne Equipment*, David & Charles, 1976

GLOSSARY

Bergmütze fur-lined ski cap
Brotbeutel bread bag
Eiergranate 'egg' hand grenade
Einheitsmütze peaked field cap
Fallschirm parachute
-**gewehr 42** assault rifle
-**helm(e)** jump helmet(s)
-**jäger** paratrooper
-**kittel** jump smock
-**Pionier(e)** engineer(s)
-**Schule** Central Parachute School
-**schützen** rifle
-**schützenabzeichen** Parachutist's Badge
-**schnürschuhe** jump boots
-**truppen** paratroops
Feldflasche mit Trinkbecher water bottle with drinking cup
Flieger flyer, flying or airborne
-**bluse** tapered-waist Flying Service Tunic
-**mütze** sidecap
Gasmaskebehälter gasmask container
Gebirgsjäger mountain trooper
Gefechtsgepäck infantry assault pack
Handschühe gauntlets
Hosen trousers
Jäger light infantryman
Kampfgruppe battlegroup
Kampfjacke Luftwaffe combat jacket

Kochgesschir mess tin
Luftaufsicht special air section
Luftlande air-landing
Mantel greatcoat
Marchstiefeln marching boots
Ofenrohr 'stovepipe'; nickname for RPzB 54
Panzerfaust 'armoured fist'; hand-held anti-tank weapon
Ritterkreuz Knight's Cross, Germany's highest military decoration
Schanzzeug entrenching spade
Schirmütze officer's peaked cap
schwere Panzerbüchse heavy anti-tank rifle
Stalhelm(e) steel helmet(s)
Stielgranate 'stick' hand grenade
Sturm assault
-**Abteilung** detachment, section or unit
-**Bataillon** battalion
-**gruppe** group (e.g. Sturmgruppe 'Granit')
-**Regiment(er)** regiment(s)
Tuchrock four-pocket Service Tunic
Waffenfarbe arm of service colour
Werkzügtasche toolboxes
Zeltbahn triangular poncho
Zug a squad

THE COLOUR PLATES

A: JÄGER, 1940

1 Helmet showing liner with straps. **2** Parachutist's jump badge. **3** Zeiss binoculars. **4** MP 40 sub-machine-gun. **5** Leather MP 40 magazine pouches. **6** Leather map case with stitched-on pockets for pencils, ruler and compasses. **7** Water bottle and drinking cup. **8** Front and rear views of the external knee pads. **9** Luger holster. **10** First pattern side-lacing jump boots showing cleated sole.

The newly promoted Oberjäger Willi Schmidt poses proudly for the camera. Although based accurately on a photograph, this portrait is anomalous and was possibly posed for a recruiting poster. Schmidt is in parade dress with shirt and tie and the blancoed canvas parachute harness neatly fastened over his jump smock. However, he would not have been festooned with personal kit while on parade, whilst by the same token the equipment would have been worn under the smock during a drop. Similarly, he is wearing jump boots instead of the standard Wehrmacht marching boots, which would usually have been worn on parade.

On his head is the Fallschirmjäger helmet painted Luftwaffe blue-grey with the national tricolour decal on one side and a silver-grey Luftwaffe eagle on the other. The detail view shows the unique liner and straps. The liner was a dome-shaped piece of leather pierced by a number of ventilation holes. It was held in position by a band of aluminium backed with resilient sorbo rubber padding which was fixed to the helmet shell by four screws which also served as anchors for the neck and chin straps. These were so designed that the helmet could not slip forward over the eyes during a drop.

On his body Schmidt is wearing a first pattern jump smock and standard combat trousers: on the right leg can be seen the pocket for the gravity knife. However, he has not donned the protective external knee pads shown in the detail view. Of similar construction to a cricket batsman's pads, the latter consisted of six horizontal tubes in black or brown leather filled with sorbo rubber which were fastened behind the knees by adjustable elasticated straps. On his hands and feet Schmidt wears black leather gauntlets and first pattern side-lacing jump boots. In his hands he carries an Erma 9mm MP (Maschinenpistole) 40 sub-machine-gun (often erroneously referred to as a 'Schmeisser' even though Hugo Schmeisser was not responsible for the design). This simple, highly effective blow-back design was issued in larger quantities to the Fallschirmtruppen than to any troops other than Panzer crews and Panzergrenadiers because of its compact size and high rate of fire (500rpm cyclic), and because the paratroops were expected to be in close contact with the enemy almost immediately after landing. Its only drawback in combat was a tendency to jam because of the inefficient single-column feed system. It had a 30-round box magazine, weighed a mere 10lb (4.7kg) and was only just over two feet (630mm) long without the folding tubular stock. Spare ammunition boxes were carried in threes in canvas or leather, or canvas and leather, pouches on the leather waist belt. In combat, it was usual to carry two spare sets, and photographs sometimes even show further sets strapped to the lower legs. Our Oberjäger Schmidt, however, has a leather map case instead, and the lightweight Zeiss 6x30 binoculars further show that he is a squad (Zug) leader. The last item of personal kit visible in the portrait is the essential water bottle plus drinking cup (Feldflasche mit Trinkbecher) behind the right hip (see also Plate G). The bottle was covered in canvas or hessian which, when wet, acted as a coolant through evaporation. Worn on the left chest of the Fliegerbluse (Flying Service Blouse), and therefore hidden by the jump smock, would be the Luftwaffe Parachutist's Badge (Fallschirmschützenabzeichen). This handsome decoration, with a gilt eagle diving across a silvered acorn and oakleaf wreath, was awarded to each recruit after six successful jumps. Those entitled to it jealously preserved it when the later, so-called 'Fallschirmjäger' units, began forming comprised largely of personnel who had never made a single one.

B: PARACHUTE JUMPING AND EQUIPMENT

The main part of the illustration (**1**) shows the Fallschirmjäger's descent. After hooking their static lines to the anchor cable in the Ju 52 the men shuffled forward on command to brace themselves in the doorway as shown in one of the photographs. At the command 'Jump!', they launched themselves in a spread-eagled position to prevent tumbling and perhaps snagging the static line; this posture also reduced the shock when the 'chute opened, at which point the men found themselves being dragged backwards until they were lying almost horizontally. After oscillating for a few seconds, the 'chute would steady and the men would begin dropping vertically (or nearly so, depending on the wind strength). Neither the RZ 1 nor RZ 16 parachute had lift webs, or 'risers', as on British and American designs, but two ropes converging into one from behind the shoulder blades. This unwieldy arrangement made it impossible to control the descent, leaving the men helpless until they were on the ground. As the ground rushed up, the jägers were forced to throw their arms forward and their legs back so as to adopt a leaning forward posture designed to help stop them getting entangled when the 'chute collapsed. Since any landing before the advent of modern skydiving 'wings' was heavy (at between 12 and 19 feet [4–6m] per second), the men would be pitched face forward the moment their boots grounded – hence the need for the knee pads and gauntlets. On the ground, the harness had to be removed as quickly as possible, a process hindered by the lack of a single central quick-release button. Then the smock had to be undone to allow the men to unbuckle and rebuckle their equipment belts and race to the nearest supply container to grab weapons and ammunition. **2** Opened out view of the RZ 1 parachute harness. Some accidents were caused by the shoulder straps slipping so on the RZ 16 harness they were further joined together across the shoulder blades by a stout canvas yoke just below the 'D' rings on to which the parachute pack itself clipped. Needless to say, everything was double stitched for strength. **3** Rear view of the RZ 1 parachute pack with the static line folded down the right-hand side. This led to an unacceptably high level of 'chute failure and on the RZ 16 the line was folded across the top of the pack. On both, however, the static line was normally carried over the left shoulder, and often clenched in the teeth to leave both hands free. The white patch on the left is simply a stores label. **4** Typical supply container. This

Although handguns were rarely useful in combat except in emergencies, they were sometimes all a Fallschirmjäger had for self-defence until he reached a weapons container. Detail is indistinct in this posed shot, but the jäger in the foreground appears to have a Walther P 38 and his companion a Luger P 08.

particular one holds an MG 34 machine-gun beneath which would be both a folded bipod and sustained fire tripod, spare barrels and boxes of 50-round 7.92mm ammunition belts plus two smaller toolboxes (Werkzügtasche). These contained a spare bolt, barrel end covers, folded anti-aircraft sight, feeder tap and other components.

C: SIDEARMS AND PERSONAL WEAPONS

Shown here (**1**) is the famous 9mm Luger P 08, the weapon being field-stripped to its component parts, the eight-round box magazine (**1a**), a standard ogival cartridge (**1b**) and a truncated cone cartridge (**1c**). George Luger developed an earlier design by Hugo Borchardt into what is probably the world's most famous sidearm, with over two million being produced in 35 variants. It was adopted by the German Army in 1908 (hence its designation) and remained in service throughout both World Wars. A common question, though, is: 'What use is a pistol in combat?' to which the facile answer is, 'Not a lot!' As a generalisation, automatic pistols or revolvers in all armies are predominantly carried as symbols of authority by officers (both commissioned and non-commissioned) and military policemen. However, they are also carried, for example, by aircrew, who would otherwise be weaponless if forced to bale out or land in enemy territory; by tank crewmen (in addition to sub-machine-guns), who would similarly be weaponless if their vehicle was disabled; and by, for further example, engineers carrying heavy loads and needing their hands free. To these categories we can add the Fallschirmtruppen, because a pistol is the only weapon that can be carried safely under a jump smock and parachute harness. For this reason, the vast majority of photographs show that jägers of all ranks wore a sidearm as a matter of course. No pistol is really of more than nuisance value much above 40–50m

(50 yards), but who would want to take a chance if it was pointing directly at them and spitting flame? For the Fallschirmjäger, therefore, a sidearm was a means in an emergency of seizing a few seconds' precious grace before grabbing a 'real' weapon from a container.

1 9mm Parabellum Pistole P 08 (Luger). Standard length 8.75in (222mm); barrel length 4.05in (103mm); unloaded weight 1.92lb (0.88kg); muzzle velocity 1,250ft/sec (391m/sec). The box magazine carries eight rounds (and it is not safe to carry an extra one 'up the spout' with a Luger). The original ammunition was the steel-jacketed, nickel-coated, truncated cone design; this contravened the Hague Convention and was replaced by the ogival pattern after 1916, which was copper coated. Both, of course, had a lead core. There is a slight upward recoil 'kick' on firing but the weapon naturally returns to the aiming position. To field strip a Luger for cleaning or maintenance, as shown, you first check it is not loaded. The barrel assembly (**1d**) is then pushed back until the toggle touches the ramp, the trigger plate locking lever turned through 90 degrees (**A**) and the plate slid forward to free the flange (**B**). The barrel can then be slid out forwards, the cross pin (**1e**) removed from the toggle and the breech block assembly slid off backwards. The pistol grips (**1f**) simply unscrew if required.

2 9mm (kurz) Parabellum Walther PP. Length 6.8in (173mm); barrel length 3.9in (99mm); unloaded weight 1.5lb (0.68kg); muzzle velocity 950ft/sec (290m/sec). Originally produced as a police weapon in 1929, the Walther PP was also issued in large numbers to the Luftwaffe (Hermann Göring, of course, controlling both forces). The Fallschirmtruppen particularly appreciated its small size and weight as well as the safety features which significantly helped reduce accidents during drops, for example. The pistol has an eight-round box magazine.

3 7.65mm Sauer-Selbsladepistole (self-loading pistol) Modell 38H. Length 6.75in (171mm); barrel length 3.27in (83mm); unloaded weight 1.56lb (0.70kg); muzzle velocity 900ft/sec (274m/sec). Although it was designed like the Walther PP as a police pistol, almost the entire production of the Sauer 38H was taken over by the Luftwaffe and, despite its small calibre and low muzzle velocity, it almost became the standard sidearm for the Fallschirmtruppen before more powerful service pistols became available in quantity. It has an eight-round box magazine.

4 9mm Pistole Automatique Browning, modèle à Grande Puissance 1935 (German designation Pistole P620[b]). Length 7.75in (196mm); barrel length 4.41in (112mm); unloaded weight 2.23lb (1.01kg); muzzle velocity 1,160ft/sec (354m/sec). The author's favourite handgun, and that of many thousands of service personnel over the years, the Browning High Power (HP) has probably been produced in greater numbers than any other service pistol and is still in widespread use decades after it first went into production with Fabrique Nationale (FN) at Liège in 1935. Its big advantage over all others until the advent of modern 'mini' sub-machine-guns was the fact that it has a 13-round box magazine compared to the normal seven or eight, which is a great reassurance to any soldier. After the Wehrmacht successfully overran Belgium in 1940, FN were ordered to keep it in production, initially for the Waffen-SS, but its advantages were so obvious and the SS at that time so small that it was soon in service with all branches of the German forces – including, of course, the Fallschirmtruppen, who especially appreciated the extra rounds of ammunition. Particularly well balanced and smooth on firing, it is very robust and hard-wearing and normally needs less cleaning than many other automatic pistols, which is a bonus in the field.

5 9mm Parabellum Walther P 38. Length 8.58in (219mm); barrel length 4.88in (124mm); unloaded weight 2.12lb (0.96kg); muzzle velocity 1,150ft/sec (350m/sec). When Hitler came to power in 1933, amongst his many military priorities was a combat pistol for the Wehrmacht which was cheaper, simpler and faster to manufacture than the venerable P 08. Walther Waffenfabrik had already produced the PP, but this was not considered to have the 'stopping power' required of a service pistol, so they began work on a new design which was issued to its first recipients in 1938. These were the Panzertruppen but the design was (and remains to this day) so successful that it was immediately in demand from all branches of the Wehrmacht and fledgling Waffen-SS. It is robust, accurate, hard-wearing and incorporates similar safety features to the PP. Unlike the Luger, a man can safely keep a round chambered because the hammer can be gently lowered on to a safety block which requires a deliberate pull on the trigger to move. The only problem some soldiers with smaller hands encounter is that the butt (containing the eight-round magazine) is rather bulky compared to that of the Luger.

6 Stielgranate ('handle grenade') M1924. Weighing 1.3lb (0.59kg) with a 0.37lb (0.17kg) warhead, the 'stick grenade' (as it is popularly known) introduced in 1924 features in almost all photos of German troops in action. It had a four-second fuse activated by unscrewing the base of the handle and pulling on the lanyard running through its core. It could be thrown to a distance of about 40yd (30–40m) and had a blast circle some 40ft (13m) in diameter. The handle itself could be unscrewed and up to seven warheads taped together around one central one to multiply the blast effect, which was particularly effective in attacking trenches or pillboxes.

7 Eiergranate ('egg grenade') M1939. The standard hand grenade with which the Fallschirmtruppen used to stuff the pockets of their jump smocks was of the high explosive fragmentation type. Weighing only 0.75lb (0.34kg) it could be thrown further than the 'stick grenade' but had a similar blast radius.

8 Bayonet Modell S84/98 and **8a** canvas and mild steel belt frog. The standard bayonet produced for use with the Mauser Gew 98 rifle and Kar 98 carbine, this was used throughout the war by all branches of the Wehrmacht and Waffen-SS. The blade was 9.92in (252mm) long and had a runnel to facilitate extraction. As with most German bayonets, the pommel was in the shape of a stylised eagle's head. Grips were of wood. During the Third Reich period the blade length was shortened slightly to 9.76in (248mm).

9 Bayonet Modell S98/04 in leather and mild steel frog. This later model, produced in smaller quantities, had the same length blade although it was slightly broader. The principal visible difference is the curved quillon and the fact that most handles were encased in bakelite instead of wood.

10 Fallschirmjäger gravity knife, see main text for description.

D: STURMGRUPPE 'GRANIT', EBEN EMAEL, 10 MAY 1940

Amongst all the achievements of the Fallschirmtruppen during the invasions of Belgium and Holland, this stands out most. The immense concrete and steel fortress of Eben Emael dominated the Albert Canal, the roads leading west from Maastricht and crucial bridges at Kanne, Vroenhoven and Veldwezelt. Eben Emael had 17 gun casemates that would have inflicted a heavy toll on conventional troops, but the bridges were essential to the German army's speedy advance, so they had to be captured and the fortress put out of action. The big question was 'How?' Against initial disbelief and hostility from the army, General Student won acceptance of his idea of using a specially trained assault force landed by glider on top of the supposedly impregnable obstacle. Gliders were chosen instead of parachutes because they could be landed more accurately and because the assault force would need cumbersome equipment, including flamethrowers, demolition charges and scaling ladders.

In November 1939 the men who were to spearhead the invasion of Belgium began assembling in great secrecy at Hildesheim. They formed Sturmabteilung 'Koch', led by Hauptmann Walter Koch, comprising 11 officers and 427 men from I and II Bataillonen of 1 Fallschirm Regiment. The group chosen for the attack on the fortress itself consisted of the 85 men of Oberleutnant Rudolf Witzig's Fallschirm-Pionier Kompanie, given the codename Sturmgruppe 'Granit'. All leave was cancelled and the group spent the best part of six months rehearsing its role, studying maps, a relief model and intelligence reports of interviews with disenchanted Belgian labourers who had worked on Eben Emael's construction. Finally, all was ready and the men of the Sturmabteilung assembled at Köln-Ostheim and Köln-Butzweilerhof airfields during the afternoon of 9 May.

Witzig's Sturmgruppe 'Granit' had been allocated 11 DFS 230 gliders, which took off behind their Ju 52 towing aircraft at 04:30 next morning. The gliders were released short of the Belgian border to glide the last 32km (20 miles) silently; the sun rising behind them making visual detection difficult. The army's main ground assault across the border was scheduled to begin five minutes after the gliders had landed to avoid alerting the defenders. Unfortunately, the tow ropes of two of the gliders, including Witzig's, parted shortly after take-off so only nine landed on the fortress, which was shrouded in early morning mist. Temporary command was assumed by Oberfeldwebel (Sergeant-Major) Helmut Wenzel, seen in this plate leading his section towards one of the gun emplacements, while behind them other jägers assault their own designated targets. Surprise was virtually complete and, although a few alert Belgian anti-aircraft machine-gunners opened fire as the gliders came in to land, there was no real opposition until shells from field artillery deployed west of the fortress began to descend on the plateau. The Belgians had not thought to protect Eben Emael against assault from the air, so there were no upright stakes to rip into the gliders, no barbed wire, no minefields and no infantry defences for the gun positions.

Wenzel's men are all wearing the same helmets (smeared with mud), smocks and jump boots as in Plate A, but note slight variations in the smocks: one man just has two hip pockets, one has a single zippered left breast pocket and Wenzel himself has two breast pockets. He also has a whistle on a cord and a small flashlight clipped to his left shoulder strap; both were standard Wehrmacht issue to junior leaders. The men carry an assortment of equipment including stick grenades tucked in their belts and ammunition bandoliers. One man has a folding assault ladder. Some of the fortress walls were over 4m (13ft) high, and the ladders had been home-made by Witzig's pioniere to exactly the right length. Another man has a Modell 40 flamethrower, a weapon that weighed nearly 50lb (21.32kg, to be precise) but could fire ten one-second bursts to a range of about 27m (30 yards). Oberfeldwebel Wenzel himself is firing his MP 40 as he runs. Behind them, two men are setting up an MG 34 while a sixth is still scrambling out of the glider. From the roof of the glider itself the pilot – who is also a fully trained Fallschirmjäger – is firing the MG 15 machine-gun, which was fitted as standard to give the paras covering fire as they deployed.

Given that the Belgians were unprepared and taken by surprise; that they were understrength because their CO, Major Jottrand, had sent many men on leave while others were billeted in nearby villages; and that they were low-grade static troops with no stomach for a firefight outside the security of their concrete walls, it is little wonder that the assault succeeded even though the Fallschirmtruppen were outnumbered ten to one. Nine gun installations were put out of action within the first ten minutes, while two turned out to be dummies that consumed precious time. By nightfall the jägers had control of the ground and dropped demolition charges down the lift shafts to prevent the garrison launching a sortie against them. At 07:00 next morning they were relieved by the army's 51 Pionier Bataillon, which crossed the Albert Canal in assault boats, and shortly afterwards Major Jottrand raised a white flag. Casualties were incredibly light. Five men were injured during the landing, 15 wounded and six killed. Witzig, who had resumed command of the operation at 08:30 on the morning of the attack after securing a second tow for his glider, was amongst those involved who were personally awarded the *Ritterkreuz* (Knights Cross) by Hitler.

E: KEEPING OUT THE COLD: BUNKER LIFE, RUSSIA 1942

Despite their losses on Crete earlier in the year, in September 1941 II Bataillon of the Luftlande-Sturm Regiment was sent to Russia, shortly followed by the bulk of 7 Flieger Division, which was renamed 1 Fallschirm Division in October the following year. During their first winter the Fallschirmtruppen were involved in the siege of Leningrad, but by their second they were further south on the Smolensk front. This plate shows a company command post during the latter period, after the Luftwaffe had begun issuing proper winter clothing. By this time the standard Wehrmacht greatcoat had proved totally inadequate and the elite formations, i.e. the Fallschirmtruppen and front-line Waffen-SS, had begun receiving more adequate protective gear. Gebirgsjäger, being intended for mountain fighting, had theirs from the beginning, but the ordinary line infantrymen had to soldier on regardless. The campaign in Russia swayed backwards and forwards in surges with long lulls in between major offensives by either side after Operation Barbarossa had run out of steam. As a result, the lines on both sides incorporated many semi-permanent fortifications designed as much to provide shelter from the elements as from enemy bombs and artillery fire, just as during the stalemate periods of the First World War.

Bunkers were dug 12–15 feet (3–4m) into the earth, sometimes deeper. The walls were shored up by rough-hewn pine or birch logs and they were roofed with felled tree trunks, above which the excavated earth was tamped back. A properly constructed bunker like the one shown could withstand direct hits by 105mm shells and gave a good measure of protection against heavier projectiles. Heating was usually achieved through the simple expedient of looting village houses of their cast iron stoves. Firewood was rarely a problem: European Russia is heavily forested and vast numbers of houses were in any case built of wood which could be ransacked. Power for lights, and for radios, came from a diesel generator, but in the event of a power failure paraffin lamps or candles sufficed, and helped provide extra warmth. Bunker floors were sometimes boarded over, but for the lower ranks were usually just hard-packed earth strewn with straw. In this sense, both winter and summer were in some respects the best times of the year, because the spring thaw and autumnal rains turned the floors into glutinous quagmires.

Furniture, such as it was, might be either looted or home-made from discarded packing cases or pallets. Bunks were packed tightly together to allow as many men as possible to sleep in the confined space (and generate body heat for each other). Weapons and outdoor clothing were kept to hand and close to the bunker entrance, which itself was protected against attack by at least one sandbagged right-angle bend and against the elements by blankets. Apart from a latrine trench dug some distance away, sanitary arrangements would normally consist of a decapitated oil drum, but since washing facilities were equally primitive, men soon learned to become oblivious of each other's odours. Officers and some men kept up an appearance of shaving, and hair on the head was always cut short to help avoid lice.

Within these harsh conditions, all ranks strove to create an environment in which they could both work efficiently and live with minimum discomfort. In this plate, one discomfort is obvious as a sentry returns from duty, bringing a blast of icy air and a flurry of snow with him to the apparent annoyance of the two officers playing 'Skat' at their makeshift table, which has been positioned as close to the stove as possible. The sentry is wearing an ordinary Wehrmacht M40 Stahlhelm instead of the Fallschirmjäger helmet; a practice which became increasingly common as the war dragged on. For protection against the intense cold outside, which limited sentry duty on occasion to 20 minutes or less, he is wearing a heavy sheepskin coat. This might have been purloined from a Russian farmer, or been donated as part of the clothing aid programme initiated by Goebbels after the first disastrous Russian winter. The sentry's weapon is the normal Mauser 7.92mm Kar 98 carbine, and other rifles and bandoliers are kept stacked close to the bunker entrance. The top two pouches on the bandolier each contained five rounds of ammunition, the lower four ten. Another officer, Schirmütze tipped over his eyes, is obliviously asleep in his cramped bunk, while the radio operator is concentrating on an incoming message. The latter is wearing a standard Fliegerbluse with the golden-yellow Fallschirmjäger Waffenfarbe, rank insignia of an Oberjäger and trade badge on his left sleeve.

The two officers playing cards, the company Captain (Hauptmann) and a 2nd Lieutenant (Leutnant), are both wearing unbuttoned (thanks to the warmth from the stove) the four-pocket Tuchrock, which many officers preferred to the Fliegerbluse. The Hauptmann has been decorated with the Iron Cross both First and Second Class, as well as the Luftwaffe Ground Assault Badge in bronze, and the 'Kreta' cuffband shows that he was involved in Operation 'Merkur'. His lieutenant only wears the ribbon of the Iron Cross Second Class, but both men proudly display the Parachutist's Badge showing they are 'real' Fallschirmtruppen rather than Johnnie-come-latelies with no jump experience. The Leutnant has donned quilted winter overtrousers and his similarly quilted jacket, with attached hood, hangs over the back of his chair.

F: ON CAMPAIGN IN THE APENNINE FOOTHILLS, ITALY 1943

In March 1943 the survivors of the re-christened 1 Fallschirm Division were grateful to find themselves entrained west away from the maelstrom of the Russian front. They re-mustered at Flers, near Avignon, France, and had a blissful three months' recuperation while their numbers were rebuilt. On 9 July, however, American and British paratroops spearheaded the invasion of Sicily and three days later I and III Bataillonen of 3 Fallschirm Regiment were airlifted to Rome. They were followed by 4 Regiment, which actually preceded them to the island in DFS 230 gliders, while 1 Regiment was held in reserve outside Naples. On 17 August, 3 and 4 Regiments were withdrawn to the mainland and 1 Fallschirm Division

spent the remainder of the war in Italy, its most famous achievement being the epic defence of Cassino.

This plate shows a typical bivouac in an olive grove in the foothills of the Apennine Mountains where an off-duty section of Fallschirmtruppen is awaiting orders. It is only a temporary encampment, evidenced by the fact that the men's sole shelter against the heat of the sun during the day and the chill in the mountains at night is a collection of *Zeltbahn* tents. The Zeltbahn was a triangular-shaped cape or poncho with a vent in the middle through which a man put his head; tapes along the edges allowed it to be fastened under the arms and at the waist, creating a draughty but rain-resistant garment which, when not needed, rolled up into a small bundle carried on the back (see also Plate G). Four Zeltbahnen could be taped together and, using an upended rifle with its bayonet in the ground as a centre-pole, a small two-man tent was made that offered only moderate discomfort. More capes could be taped together in alternate fashion to create a low ridge tent.

Rifles are shown stacked where they can be grabbed easily, and in the foreground of the illustration is a little 2.8cm sPzB 41 (*schwere Panzerbüchse*, or heavy anti-tank rifle, Modell 1941). The latter was a 'squeeze' or tapered bore weapon developed during 1941 and introduced into service in 1942 in response to demands from the front-line troops for a more effective light anti-tank gun than the 3.7cm PaK 35/36. Despite the fact that the latter continued to soldier on until at least 1944, it was obsolescent even before the outbreak of war and quickly earned itself the nickname *Türklingel* (doorbell) because it was so ineffective against enemy tanks. The sPzB 41 was the smallest of three main tapered bore anti-tank guns developed during the war from earlier studies and experiments by Hermann Gerlich. In each case, the gun barrel tapered smoothly or in stages so that the muzzle had a smaller diameter than the breech. The projectile casing fitted the breech, but the shot itself had studs, fins or a driving band which compressed as the high explosive over-charge propelled it down the barrel, resulting in an incredibly high muzzle velocity. In the case of the sPzB 41, this was 3,572ft/sec (1,402m/sec) compared with that of Germany's most successful ordinary anti-tank gun, the 7.5cm PaK 40, which was only 2,590ft/sec (792m/sec). With solid shot, as contrasted to hollow charge or 'squash head' rounds, the weight and density of the projectile are as important as its velocity, so sPzB 41 shot was made of tungsten. Unfortunately for Germany, supplies of the ore wolfram, from which tungsten is extracted, were already running low by the time the tapered bore weapons entered service, so comparatively few were manufactured. For the Fallschirmtruppen, however, while the ammunition lasted the sPzB 41 was a veritable godsend. It could easily be dropped by parachute, the whole gun on the airborne carriage shown here weighing only 260lb (118kg). It could be moved and operated single-handed, although a crew of three was normal because of the weight of the ammunition boxes as much as anything else. It was also very accurate and could disable an Allied M4 Sherman at over 500 yards (500m).

Of more antique vintage is the little mule supply cart, 'borrowed' from Italian villagers, being unloaded in the encampment in the olive grove. The two jägers tending it wear a casual mixture of tropical clothing, also emulated by the Oberleutnant and Feldwebel (1st Lieutenant and Sergeant) studying their map in the foreground of the illustration. Both men are wearing tropical shirts without

Nine men from Sturmabteilung Koch were personally awarded the Ritterkreuz by a delighted Hitler. From left to right they are Leutnant Egon Delica, Oberleutnant Rudolf Witzig, Hauptmann Walter Koch, Oberleutnant Otto Zierach, Leutnant Helmuth Ringler, Leutnant Joachim Meissner, Oberleutnant Walter Kiess, Oberleutnant Gustav Altmann and Oberarzt Dr Rolf Jäger, the team's doctor.

insignia apart from shoulder boards and chest eagle, colourful silk scarves which had become something of a Fallschirmjäger trademark, tropical issue trousers and second pattern front-lacing jump boots. The pipe-smoking Feldwebel with the injured arm has a tropical pattern Einheitsmütze for protection against the sun's glare and wears a holstered Luger on his waist belt. However, it is not a standard Luger but the so-called 'artillery model', the Luger *Lange* Pistole '08. Over 200,000 of these were produced during the First World War and there were still large numbers around in the 1940s. Those lucky enough to acquire one appreciated the greater muzzle velocity and accuracy conferred by the 8in (200mm) barrel with its rear sight. Note also the difference between the belt plate worn by enlisted men and NCOs and the buckle on the officer's belt.

The Oberleutnant wears a buttoned second-pattern jump smock which lacked the legs of the first pattern that had caused so much inconvenience. On a jump, the lower halves of this garment simply buttoned around the upper legs,

making it much easier to gain access to the equipment belt after landing. Photographs show the smock in action being worn both buttoned fully and unbuttoned, with or without an equipment belt. The Oberleutnant's headgear is the popular 'Meyer' cap, nicknamed after an obscure and not very funny reference to Göring's boast that if an enemy bomb ever fell on Berlin he was to be known as 'Hermann Meyer'. That aside, it was a very practical cap in lightweight material with a barely stiffened peak, clearly defining an officer yet offering a great deal of comfort. The soft brown leather chinstrap was usually worn as shown except in a high wind, and the detachable neck flap appears from photographs to have been worn rarely.

PLATE G: LEUTNANT, ARDENNES, DECEMBER 1944

Having risen through the ranks and been sent to officer training school after a field promotion to Leutnant, Schmidt is a changed man from the confident, arrogant teenager seen in Plate A. Five years of war have aged him, dark rings under his bloodshot eyes betray countless sleepless nights and he has not managed to shave today. His uniform and equipment have also altered radically and, although some of this is for the better, it will not help stop Patton's U.S. Third Army as it counter-attacks through 5 Fallschirm Division toward Bastogne at Christmas.

As an 'old hand', Schmidt retains the Fallschirmjäger jump helmet while newer members of the two Fallschirm divisions involved in the Ardennes offensive, largely drafted from other Luftwaffe formations, wore the standard Stahlhelm. His helmet is covered by a string net into which leaves and twigs could be inserted to break up the silhouette, and he wears a woollen toque. Jump smocks had, however, disappeared to a degree by this stage of the war except for special operations such as 'Stösser', the abortive attempt by a Fallschirmjäger kampfgruppe led by Oberst Friedrich Freiherr von der Heydte to secure an important road junction behind American lines at the beginning of the 'Battle of the Bulge'. Schmidt therefore wears the combat jacket in splinter camouflage material which was first issued to the Luftwaffe field divisions in 1942. His trousers, however, are the padded type made of a cotton/rayon mix in the brownish water pattern camouflage which was also used on the 'third pattern' jump smocks. In place of the earlier vents in the side through which to withdraw the internal knee pads, these have a flap fastened by a plastic press stud. Jump boots are something else which had almost disappeared by 1944 but Schmidt still has a second pattern pair, gaitered at the ankle for reinforcement and, presumably, a tiny extra bit of warmth. Both the insignia on the collar of his Fliegerbluse and the cloth patch on his arm denote his rank. Together with his officer's pattern waist belt he wears the full infantry assault pack (Gefechtsgepäck) which carried the mess tin (Kochgesschir), rolled Zeltbahn, bread bag (Brotbeutel), entrenching spade (Schanzzeug) with its Luftwaffe blue-grey cover, water bottle (see also Plate A) and gas respirator container (Gasmaskebehälter). It should be noted that, by this stage of the war, neither side really expected the other to use poison gases, so this handy metal container probably contains washing and shaving kit or other personal items. The same pair of now rather battered binoculars hang round his neck alongside a torch, but he is carrying a different weapon, an FG (Fallschirmgewehr) 42 assault rifle.

The FG 42 was one of the most remarkable weapons of the war and, although only about 7,000 were manufactured due to its complexity and cost, its gas-operated mechanism, and the open/closed bolt system which allowed for single-shot or automatic fire, have been copied in most post-war automatic rifles. The story of its genesis is far too long to go into here, but it was inspired by the usual rivalry between the Heer, which had introduced the world's first self-loading automatic rifle in the form of the Haenel/Schmeisser 7.92mm (kurz) MP 43/StG 44, and the Luftwaffe, which wanted one of its own for the Fallschirmtruppen. The result was a very light (10lb/4.5kg) weapon with a straight line barrel-to-butt layout, sloping pistol grip (later discarded because of cost in favour of a more conventional pistol grip), ergonomically designed plastic shoulder butt, integral bipod for use in the light machine-gun role, muzzle flash eliminator and even a special 'spike' bayonet rather like an ice pick. The weapon's only real drawback in use was the side-mounted 20-round box magazine, which unbalanced it unless the bipod was used and tended to snag on relatively loose clothing such as the jump smock. Its main advantage in the field compared with the MP 43/StG 44 was that it used the same long 7.92mm cartridge as in the standard Gew/Kar 98 rifle and carbine, so reloading the magazine was never the problem it was in the early days of the army rifle.

1 FG 42 showing box magazine (**1a**) and spike bayonet (**1b**). **2** Infantry assault pack as described above. The only item normally worn which is omitted in this case because of

the FG 42 rifle is a bayonet frog (see Plate C). **3** 15cm Panzerfaust 60. Even before supplies of tungsten for the sPzB 41 ran out, other designers had been working on the same problem of providing front-line infantry – including the Fallschirmtruppen – with a light but effective anti-tank weapon. The first practical design to emerge in 1943 from the Hugo Schneider factory in Leipzig was the Panzerfaust ('armoured fist') 30, which went into production in October that year at the incredible rate of 200,000 a month. However, production had to be cheap and quick because it was a 'throw away' design which could only be used once. A simple hollow steel tube contained an explosive propellant charge, a percussion firing mechanism and a primitive sight; the sight acted as a safety catch protecting the firing button from being depressed accidentally. Into the front end slotted a 15 cm (5.9in) diameter bomb whose stem was fitted with flexible fins which unfolded in flight. The range with the first models was only 30m (33 yards) but the 1.5kg (3.31lb) hollow-charge Cyclonite/TNT warhead could penetrate 140mm (5.5in) of armour plate sloped at 30 degrees – more than enough to ruin any Allied tank man's day, although of course it required great courage to get that close. After firing, the tube was discarded. The second version illustrated here emerged in the summer of 1944 and, while retaining the same basic design, had a larger propellant charge and was sighted to 60m (67yd). Both weapons' biggest disadvantage in action was that their back-blast invariably gave away the firer's position, but they were quite rightly feared by Allied tank crews, who learned in the Ardennes not to try to operate at night. The Panzerjäger ('tank hunter') companies in German infantry regiments alone carried 54 Panzerfausts, enough to knock out an entire American tank battalion! **4** 8.8cm RPzB 54 (Racketen Panzerbüchse [rocket anti-tank rifle] Modell 54). Nicknamed 'Ofenrohr' ('stovepipe') by the troops, this was the most effective infantry anti-tank weapon of the whole war. American bazookas captured in North Africa after Operation 'Torch' in November 1942 provided the inspiration, but German designers improved on the original by increasing the warhead diameter from 60 to 88mm (2.36 to 3.45in) since with any hollow-charge device it is diameter which is all-important. (Velocity is irrelevant and, in fact, high velocity actually impairs performance, hence the trend towards smoothbore guns in modern main battle tanks.) This was still less than the diameter of the Panzerfaust warhead, and the explosive charge only weighed 0.66kg (1.45lb), but it could penetrate 100mm (4in) of tank armour and the range was a much more realistic 120m (130yd). Early versions lacked the simple blast shield shown, forcing the user to wear a gas respirator to protect his face. Unlike the Panzerfaust, the RPzB 54 was not a 'throw away' weapon, but could be reloaded with one of the rocket projectiles shown (**4a**). It was ignited by an electrical discharge from a magneto in the trigger/grip mechanism – a further improvement on the American bazooka which relied on potentially unreliable batteries – and it had a simple tubular shoulder stock to make aiming easier and more accurate. The 'stovepipe' needed a crew of two, one to carry it with its simple shoulder strap, aim and fire it, and a second to carry and reload the projectiles. Being more complex, and therefore more time-consuming and costly to manufacture than the Panzerfaust, however, the RPzB 54 was never available in sufficiently large quantity to have any decisive effect on events.

INDEX

Figures in **bold** refer to illustrations